Best
TEA SHOP WALKS
IN NORFOLK

Norman & June Buckley

Published by Sigma Leisure – an imprint of
Sigma Press, 1 South Oak Lane, Wilmslow, Cheshire SK9 6AR, England.

British Library Cataloguing in Publication Data
A CIP record for this book is available from the British Library.

ISBN: 1-85058-702-7

Typesetting and Design by: Sigma Press, Wilmslow, Cheshire.

Cover photographs: *main picture* – Elm Hill, Norwich; *smaller pictures, from top* – Cley Mill; Norwich Cathedral; Coltishall; Oxburgh Hall. All supplied by Ikon Imaging, Norwich.

Photographs within the book: the authors

Maps: Jeremy Semmens

Printed by: MFP Design and Print

Disclaimer: the information in this book is given in good faith and is believed to be correct at the time of publication. No responsibility is accepted by either the author or publisher for errors or omissions, or for any loss or injury howsoever caused. Only you can judge your own fitness, competence and experience.

Preface

When considering the compilation of books of recommended walks, Norfolk is not an area which comes immediately to mind. The Lake District, the Peak District, the Cotswolds and others all need no prior thought; their reputations as good walking country are long established and are beyond question.

But, in recent years, a great deal of effort has gone into widening the appeal of Norfolk as a visitor destination. This effort has included the promotion of walking as a viable and enjoyable activity throughout the county. The countryside team of the county council's Planning and Transportation Department, often in association with the Countryside Commission, has been involved in the establishment of designated paths, long and short, and many parishes have recommended circular walks in their areas, subsequently collated by the county council. Waymarking of footpaths is now very good and there is little evidence of obstruction by farmers or others. Likewise, Forest Enterprises, successors to the Forestry Commission, are very walker friendly, creating many waymarked routes through their holdings such as Thetford Forest.

For these various reasons, there is now no hesitation whatsoever in recommending Norfolk to walkers.

Landscape and Walking

Of course, the landscape is less dramatic than that in some of the other areas mentioned above. There are no Scafell Pikes, no Mam Tors and not even a Cleeve Hill; the highest ground at about 100 metres is a laughable altitude to those dedicated to hill walking. In 'Lakeland Walking on the Level', the first book of the 'Level Walks' series (published by Sigma Leisure) the author, in explaining and justifying the title, made the statement 'whatever next, hillwalking in East Anglia?' That would, as the statement was intended to show, obviously be attempting the impossible but, contrary to general belief, Norfolk does go up and down. There is also an attractive coastline, much of it highly characterful. Whilst the area covered by the Broads is obviously flat, the numerous reed-fringed lakes, the sinuously winding rivers, the vast skies and the lonely wind pumps all combine to provide a landscape which many will find highly appealing.

At least equally important, the flint and mellow brick villages, often with great churches established from the wealth of the medieval wool trade, contribute to many of the selected walks. The proliferation of nature reserves, many of them of national status, with a fine range of plants, waterfowl and other wildlife, is an added bonus.

So, there is something here for the great majority of walkers, quietly satisfying rather than dramatic and, with the walks at 2 – 8 miles in length, catering at the more leisurely end of the scale. There is obviously no scrambling or rocky ground and the footpath surfaces in Norfolk are well above average, not least in being predominantly dry, quick draining and free of mud. The gentle character of the walking is such that, despite the author's well-aired views on footwear, it has to be admitted that boots are not always essential for these walks; many walkers will be comfortable in stout shoes or even trainers, particularly in dry weather. Perhaps surprisingly, a compass is occasionally useful when crossing prairie-like fields.

Designated Footpaths

Peddars Way – from Knettishall Heath near Thetford to Holme next the Sea, where it joins the **Norfolk Coast Path** from Hunstanton to Cromer. The two are now regarded as one path, with a total length of 93 miles. The Peddars Way follows the line of an ancient trackway, used by the Iceni tribe before being taken over and improved by the invading Romans as part of a route from Colchester to the Wash and probably beyond. Included in walks 3 and 28.

Norfolk Coast Path – Hunstanton to Cromer. Joins Peddars Way at Holme next the Sea; Weavers' Way and Paston Way at Cromer. Included in walks 5, 6, 7, 9 and 12.

Weavers' Way – Great Yarmouth to Cromer. Joins Norfolk Coast Path and Paston Way at Cromer. Included in walks 15, 19 and 22.

Nar Valley Way – Kings Lynn to Gressenhall. Joins Peddars Way at Castle Acre. Included in walk 28.

Paston Way – North Walsham to Cromer, focusing particularly on sixteen parish churches. Joins Norfolk Coast Path and Weavers Way at Cromer. Included in walk 13.

Bure Valley Walk – Aylsham to Hoveton by the side of the Bure Valley Railway. Joins Marriott's Way at Aylsham. Included in walk 20.

Marriott's Way – Aylsham to Reepham and extension to Norwich on former railway lines. Joins Bure Valley Walk at Aylsham. Included in walk 18.

Maps

The sketch plans and the text combine to give adequate route information but there is nothing to beat the 1:25,000 Ordnance Survey maps for putting flesh on the bones and widening the interest of the walk. The transition from the traditional small 'Pathfinder' sheets to the newer and better value for money 'Explorer' range of large sheets is proceeding apace, but there are several of the walks in the book which are still not covered and the appropriate 'Pathfinder' has to be suggested in these cases.

Tea Shops

As always in this series, the choice of suitable tea shops goes hand in hand with the walks. There is no need for hesitation in this regard. The county is well provided with the kind of towns and some villages in which one or more good tea shops is to be expected. The usual efforts have been made to diversify; stately homes, forest visitor centre, craft centre, railway station, windmill and forge all contribute to the rich array. Whilst some of the premises function purely as tea shops, the majority offer more substantial and varied catering, of which details are given in each case. Not all these premises will be open throughout the year and dates and hours do change from time to time, often at short notice. Telephone numbers are given for up to date information.

In setting out each walk, the intention has been to follow our usual practice of placing the tea shop part way round the circuit whenever practicable. Just a few walks have the tea shop at the end.

Book Layout

The book follows the well tried and tested format of presenting a few salient characteristics as an introduction to each walk, making a decision on suitability or otherwise for any particular persons or occasion a quick and simple matter. Accepting that, in some cases, the presence or otherwise of stiles can make or break the attraction of a route, appropriate comment is now included in this section. 'About the Area' is a succinct commentary on the features of the landscape, towns, villages and features such as visitor attractions which might add interest to each walk.

Norman and June Buckley

Contents

Introduction

Landscape and Geology	1
Human impact	2
The Rural Scene	3
Heritage and Tourism	3

The Walks

1. Sandringham Country Park — 5

Length: 3¼ miles

2. Snettisham — 9

Length: 5¼ miles or 3½ miles

3. Great Bircham — 14

Length: 7¼ miles (shorter versions possible)

4. North Creake — 19

Length: 4 miles

5. Burnham Market — 23

Length: 5¾ miles

6. Brancaster — 28

Length: 5¼ miles

7. Wells-next-the-Sea   32
Length: 5¾ miles

8. Little Walsingham and Great Snoring   36
Length: 5 miles

9. Blakeney and Cley-next-the-Sea   41
Length: 5½ miles

10. Holt   45
Length: 5 miles.

11. Sheringham Park   49
Length: 3¾ miles or 5½ miles

12. Pretty Corner and Beeston Priory   54
Length: 4½ miles

13. Overstrand   59
Length: 3 miles

14. Baconsthorpe   63
Length: 3¾ miles

15. Aldborough   68
Length: 5¼ miles

16. Mannington Estate   73
Length: 3 miles

17. Heydon   77
Length: 2¼ miles

18. Reepham   81
Length: 8 miles

19. Blickling Hall   86
Length: 6 miles

20. Coltishall and the Bure Valley   90
Length: 4¼ miles with return by train. (8 miles if walked both ways)

21. Ludham   94
Length: 5½ miles

22. Potter Heigham   99
Length: 5½ miles

23. Horsey Mill   103
Length: 5 miles

24. Stokesby   107
Length: 4¼ miles

25. Filby   111
Length: 2¾ miles

26. Wymondham   115
Length: 3 miles in total (1½ miles each section)

27. Thetford Forest   122
Length: 5½ miles

28. Castle Acre   126
Length: 6 miles or 7 miles

29. Oxburgh Hall   130
Length: Variable – 2½ miles maximum

30. Downham Market   134
Length: 6¾ miles.

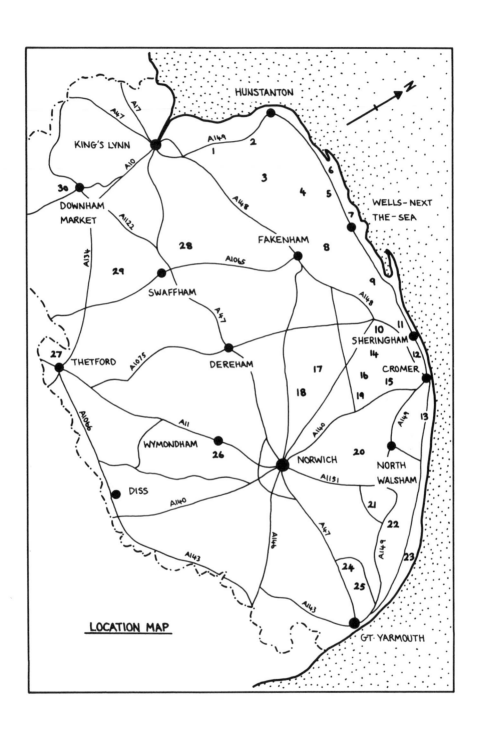

LOCATION MAP

Introduction

Landscape and Geology

Bulging out into the North Sea, flanked by a long coastline, the predominantly low-lying land which makes up East Anglia has always been a water-dominated landscape. Rivers have never flowed swiftly and purposefully to the sea; they crawl along as if reluctant to give up their waters to the flat, marshy, estuaries, traditionally subject to flooding in prolonged or violent wet weather. From Roman times much energy, time and money has gone into elaborate schemes of drainage, winning back thousands of rich alluvial acres from the water.

More dramatic is the sea's confrontation with the coast, which is largely vulnerable with, at best, low, crumbling, cliffs. Here, the conflict takes two forms. Firstly there is the constant erosion, the creeping destruction caused by the ceaseless pounding at dunes, soft cliffs and modern sea defences, possessing land, villages and the occasional town over the centuries. The prime example is Dunwich, which is in Suffolk and therefore outside the scope of this book, progressively reduced from a considerable town, Bishopric and major port to the present minor village by this elemental power. Secondly, the unfortunate combination of tides and winds can produce the 'North Sea Surge', with enormous tidal waves bursting through the defences, as in 1953 when much low-lying land in East Anglia was flooded, with great loss of life and property.

There is, however, a certain amount of give and take in the relationship between land and sea. Over a long period of time, silting has extended the North Norfolk coast into the Wash; former little ports such as Blakeney and Cley-next-the-Sea are now some distance inland. Similarly, the large town and port of Great Yarmouth has been built on a spit of land which has grown steadily since medieval times.

The final element in this watery landscape is the Norfolk (and Suffolk) Broads. Extensive digging of peat for fuel from Anglo-Saxon times to the early 14th century produced shallow but wide pits which, inevitably, flooded, producing the series of lakes and their connecting waterways which play a large part in today's Norfolk holiday economy.

On the whole, Norfolk is not noted for spectacular geology. There are no thrusting mountain ranges, no glens, ravines or similar landscape features. Apart from the cliffs at Hunstanton, all is quietly understated. Most noteworthy is a broad band of chalk which crosses southern England diagonally, from Dorset to those cliffs at Hunstanton, producing a gently rolling countryside which, in Norfolk, reaches a maximum height of about 100 metres. To the west of the chalk lie some of the oldest East Anglian strata, beds of Gault, Greensand and Kimmeridge Clay, whilst to the east Red Crag and Forest Beds have deposits of the Pliocene Age, including historically valuable sea shells.

Human impact

Despite the threats posed by water, the area has long proved attractive to man. In pre-historic times access to this isolated area from the rest of England was difficult; the great watery barrier of the fens extended south from Lincolnshire almost as far as today's Cambridge, whilst most of what is now Essex was covered in dense forest. The most attractive route was to use the chalk ridge to infiltrate into Breckland. Here, forest was relatively easy to clear and the light, sandy soil was easier to work than the heavy clays elsewhere in the area. This became one of the country's most densely populated areas, with crop growing and cattle grazing to excess over the centuries producing a heath area vulnerable to sand storms and overpopulated by rabbits. This state of affairs was not remedied until the 20th century, with the arrival of the Forestry Commission and mass planting of trees for commercial purposes. A very early industry, digging out and shaping flints, developed at Grimes Graves. In pre-historic times these were used as tools and weapons; in medieval times they became an important local building material.

Well before the arrival of the Romans, the population had become organised into tribes; because of Boadicea's rebellion against the Romans, the Iceni were the best known of these. Following the departure of the Romans, waves of Angle, Saxon and Jute invaders crossed the North Sea to arrive on the accessible shores, settling throughout the area, developing agriculture, building churches, often with distinctive round towers, and burying special chieftains in great splendour, as at Sutton Hoo in Suffolk.

Despite the exploits of Hereward the Wake, the Norman Conquest eventually prevailed in East Anglia. Churches were now built in Norman style, often modifying the earlier Anglo-Saxon buildings, and the whole area thrived, so much so that at the time of the Domesday Book the population density was among the highest in England.

The Rural Scene

The greatest landscape changes, however, occurred some centuries later when the work of Vermuyden and others brought about enormous enhancement of the drainage of the still very extensive fen areas, straightening rivers, digging long, wide, drainage channels and pumping water from lower lying fields into these channels. This achievement enabled agricultural pioneers such as Coke at Holkham and 'Turnip' Townshend of Raynham to transform much of Norfolk into probably the richest farming area in Britain, in the former case substituting wheat for the prevailing rye. There was also a side benefit in that navigation to inland ports such as Wisbech, Peterborough and Bedford was much improved.

The small fields, many of which had been 'enclosed' long before the 19th-century Parliamentary Enclosure Acts, have been expanded in the present century by much destruction of old hedges, creating 'prairies' which enable large and expensive agricultural machinery to function more efficiently.

Heritage and Tourism

Prior to the 18th-century agricultural reform, the sheep had ruled the East Anglian economy for some centuries, generating great wealth for many merchants. 'Wool' towns and villages competed in displaying this wealth, most usually by building churches of great stature and richly carved flamboyance, permanent monuments to a prosperous age. In creating monuments and, even more so, in the proliferation of vernacular architecture, the builders of Norfolk have left a wealth of distinctive features and techniques which add immeasurably to the attraction of so many of the town and villages. That awkward local material flint is at the very heart of the construction of the churches both great and small and also of many less exalted buildings.

Although for centuries Norwich was second only to London as England's largest city, the rural traditions of Norfolk, coupled with the absence of coal or iron ore deposits, hence no industrial revolution, have discouraged the development of large cities and towns. Norwich, Great Yarmouth and Kings Lynn are the biggest settlements, but are of comparatively modest size, organically grown as an integral part of their environment rather than 'foreign' intrusions as a modern industrial city might be. They are all full of visitor interest; Norwich is counted among England's great heritage places as, indeed, are some of the smaller towns and villages, whilst seaside resorts such as Hunstanton, Sheringham, and Cromer, fulfil a different kind of holiday need.

Perhaps because of the relative scarcity of polluting industry and the wide open spaces, wildlife has always been abundant, the Fens, the Broads and the coast being particularly famous for water fowl. This has been recognised by the creation of numerous reserves, some of national and even international importance.

In recent years, encouraged and promoted by an active Tourist Board, visitor attractions have increased in number, for example, farms and vineyards have opened their premises to the public, walking and cycle trails have been created, whilst Tourist Information Centres have increased their assistance to the public, including the provision of accommodation booking services in most cases.

It all adds up to an area of distinctive overall character yet, within that character, a wide diversity of landscape, of buildings and of monuments, with complimentary activities available to suit virtually any visitor.

1. Sandringham Country Park

Length:	3¼ miles
Summary:	An enjoyable stroll through part of the large area of woodland and parkland adjacent to Sandringham House. The conditions underfoot are so good that boots are hardly necessary for this walk, although one portion has a sharp little descent and later ascent, both helped by the provision of informal steps. If desired, this portion can be avoided, with consequent shortening of the circuit. There are no stiles.
Car Parking:	Good free woodland car park, not signposted. Situated in the angle between two roads towards the south end of the Country Park. Follow the signs for the more northerly of the two caravan sites (Camping and Caravaning Club). The entrance to the car park is along an unmade track between the caravan site entrance and the crossroads. Grid reference 682275.
Maps:	Ordnance Survey Explorer 23, Norfolk Coast West, 1:25,000 Ordnance Survey Landranger 132, NorthWest Norfolk, 1:50,000

Tea Shops

There are two tea options at the Visitor Centre. One is the self-service restaurant – large, smart, well-maintained and architecturally interesting. The alternative is the much smaller waitress service tea room. We choose the latter but many of the menu items are common to both. The tea room menu offers the Sandringham cream tea or one can order sandwiches, scones with jam and cream, or cakes, with tea or coffee. Savouries offered included smoked salmon salad, game pie, or ploughman's lunch. 'Brunch' comprises orange juice, Danish pastry, bacon sandwich, and coffee or tea. Note that hot food is served in the tea room only between 11.30am and 2.30pm. There is a limited amount of seating in a sunny, sheltered, outdoor area to one side of the tea room.

Open 10am to 5.30pm every day to end of November and weekends only in the winter months. Tel. 01485 544776.

About the Area

The Sandringham Estate occupies one of the prime landscape areas of north Norfolk, heavily wooded and with sufficient rise and fall to add interest. The House and its immediate gardens, together with a motor museum and the Stables refreshment block, are confined within a boundary wall. Payment is required for entry to this interesting visitor attraction, which many will no doubt wish to combine with this walk. The estate was purchased by Edward, Prince of Wales (later King Edward VII) in the mid 19th century, at the time of his marriage. The existing house was demolished, making way for the present house to be built in the Tudor style. The much restored little church of St Mary Magdalen, enriched by royal brasses and many other internal features, is also open to the public. Most of the extensive parkland is available for unrestricted wandering and the car parking provision in the estate is generous.

The visitor centre has information, shop, plant sales, tea room, self service restaurant, picnic area, adventure playground and public conveniences, including facilities for the disabled. The route below traverses a good cross section of the estate.

The Walk

Walk from the car park to the road and turn right, to go the crossroads. Turn left and, in 30 metres, fork right along a wide, sandy, track. A yellow marker can be seen to the right. Continue through the pleasant woodland of Brick Kiln Covert, with pines on the left and silver birch on the right, soon going slightly uphill.

Cross the public road to 'Country Park – scenic drive and picnic areas'. The route follows the tarmac roadway, but with wide grass verges on either side. To the right is Wild Wood as another major trail joins our route from the right. Just before a picnic area another trail goes off to the right, direct to the Visitor Centre and tea shop.

The 'scenic roadway' continues ahead, but to visit Jocelyn's Wood Nature Reserve we turn left, descending, with an area of more open country to the left. Go down some informal steps; the nearby main road is increasingly apparent as we bear right to continue along a well-used path roughly parallel with the road. Ignore any lesser paths and walk for nearly half a mile before bending steadily to the right, soon climbing beside a tiny stream. Ascend informal steps, close to an observation hide, and cross the tarmac of the 'scenic drive' to enter woodland amongst massed rhododendrons. Rejoin

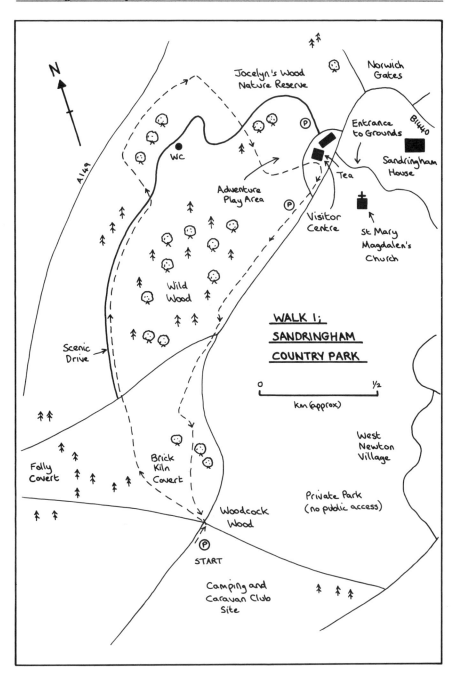

N

Jocelyn's Wood
Nature Reserve

Norwich
Gates

B1440

Entrance
to Grounds

WC

Sandringham
House

A149

Adventure
Play Area

Tea

St Mary
Magdalen's
Church

Visitor
Centre

Wild
Wood

**WALK 1;
SANDRINGHAM
COUNTRY PARK**

Scenic
Drive

0   ½
km (approx)

West
Newton
Village

Folly
Covert

Brick
Kiln
Covert

Private Park
(no public access)

Woodcock
Wood

P
START

Camping and
Caravan Club
Site

another major track and continue past the adventure playground to the visitor centre.

After refreshments, walk across grass away from the visitor centre towards car parking areas and a road with 'Kings Lynn and Hunstanton' sign. Before reaching that road turn right into a lesser road and then left in a few metres to take a woodland trail which stays parallel with the more important road for about 600 metres. There are blue and yellow paint blobs on a tree.

Look out carefully for a left fork by a 'dog fouling' bin and post and then, in another 40 metres, go left again by a second 'dog fouling' post to continue to a road, close to a junction with our original road. Go straight across this second road to a wide grassy area, beside the original road. Keep to the right of a roadside belt of trees (yellow marker on reverse side of stump) and walk along a broad grassy sward, more or less parallel with the road.

Opposite a seat on the right of the sward turn left through the trees (yellow marker on reverse side of stump), pass a grass car parking area, and descend gently through a delightful open glade with a small overgrown pond, full of tadpoles in the spring. Bear to the left as a road is approached, to rejoin the start of the walk. Turn left at the road to go to the crossroads, then turn right and, in a few metres, left into the car park.

Sandringham – for those who don't want to walk!

2. Snettisham

Length:	5¼ miles (shorter version 3½ miles).
Summary:	A varied and attractive walk including Snettisham and Ingoldisthorpe, more uphill and down dale than is usual in Norfolk but without steep ascents. Good paths through woodland, farmland and a small amount of residential area. Several stiles; none particularly difficult. Very little walking on roads.
Car Parking:	For the full version, there is a suitable car park at the south end of Snettisham Common, reached by turning towards Snettisham Beach from the A149, then into an opening on the right in 300 metres. Grid reference 673336. *For the shorter walk, park centrally in Snettisham, the little 'square' close to the tea shop is as good as anywhere.*
Maps:	Ordnance Survey Explorer 23, Norfolk Coast West, 1:25,000. Ordnance Survey Landranger 132, NorthWest Norfolk, 1:50,000.

Tea Shop

The Old Bank is a coffee shop by day and a bistro in the evening – an ideal combination. This is a particularly good place for tea with a welcome for walkers from the friendly staff. Furnishing and crockery are of a high standard, whilst reassuringly the floor is 'boot friendly'. A choice of coffee and tea is available – do try the house blend leaf tea which was specially blended by Mastins of Norwich to celebrate the Queen Mother's 80th birthday and still going strong (no pun intended!) many years later. Other varieties include Earl Grey, Darjeeling, or fruit teas. Choice of sandwiches including chicken, crab, or – more unusual – Brie with grapes, walnut and celery. Throughout the day the breakfast grill is served or, for something special, try the luxurious scrambled eggs on toast with smoked salmon. Cakes and scones are of good quality. Should you return to sample the evening offerings note this is an unlicensed restaurant so just bring your own wine – no corkage charge.

Open: 10am – 4pm daily (5pm on Saturdays and Sundays). Closed all day every Wednesday. Evening meals from 6pm – advisable to book. Tel. 01485 544080.

The Tea Shop at Snettisham

About the Area

At first sight Snettisham and Ingoldisthorpe seem to be a little anonymous, each an old nucleus expanded in recent times by over-large residential suburbs, all by-passed by the A149. But, along the main street, Snettisham has a range of shops, including a cluster round the tiny former Market Place, and a few nice old buildings generally. Ingoldisthorpe has a tucked-away church in a pleasant area uphill from the A149, Lynn Road. The comparatively high wooded area between Snettisham and the sea carries a variety of names. It is all very pleasant woodland and the path along the western edge has views to the Wash.

Park Farm, Snettisham, lies on the route, a considerable visitor attraction with paddocks containing deer and unusual breeds of farm animals. Snettisham watermill, not open to the public, is an unexpected discovery by the side of the track. The high-spired church at Snettisham is basically 13th century but has suffered reductions in size during the ensuing 600 years. Despite lowering of the roof, the interior still retains a fine impression of height and space. Flint built Ingoldisthorpe church is said to be the third building on the site; the present structure is of the 13th, 14th and 15th centuries, with an octagonal Norman font. Near the church door there is the base of an ancient cross.

The Walk

From the recommended car park go up a broad sandy track into the attractive woodland of Snettisham Common. Ignore any minor paths on the right to stay close to the left-hand edge; there are soon open views to the Wash . At a major junction keep straight on. As Lodge Hill Farm is approached, with an obvious farm gate, turn right uphill through a kissing gate into woodland and continue for about two thirds of a mile along a well-used path., ignoring any paths to right or left.

On reaching the main road, the A149, go straight across to a kissing gate and a 'public path' sign. A waymarked stile gives access to a meadow. Cross a little bridge to head for the far right-hand corner. Go through a kissing gate into a residential road. Turn left to walk past the post office to the main street (Lynn Road).

Turn right to reach the tea shop in 60 metres. Leave the tea shop by continuing along the main street; bear left in 30 metres, passing through road bollards. Pass the front of the Snettisham First School and turn right into Manor Lane. Turn left, still on Manor Lane, now with good views of the parish church. The route soon becomes a footpath, rising gently between hedges.

About 30 metres before reaching a public road turn right along a gravelled driveway. Turn right again in 10m to go through a small kissing gate on the left. Waymarks now point the way past some of the Park Farm paddocks to reach a wide trackway. Just before this track bends to the left, turn right down a grassy path, passing in front of a few cottages. As more modern houses are reached, turn left into Park Close and make for a stile and 'public footpath' signpost in the right-hand corner. Take the grass path, fenced on both sides, which leads to a stream on the far side of the field. The fenced route continues to the left, roughly following the line of the stream, rich in wild iris. Ingoldisthorpe church tower is now in view. At a junction bear left, away from a footbridge.

By a 'conservation walks' notice go right to cross a footbridge with a stile at the far end. Rise across a small, buttercup filled, meadow, keeping fairly close to the fence on the right, to head for a stile at the far end, then a kissing gate which leads to a minor public road.

Turn right to walk as far as Shernborne Road. To visit the church (which may well be closed), turn left and then left again to take a path on the left which is signposted to the church.

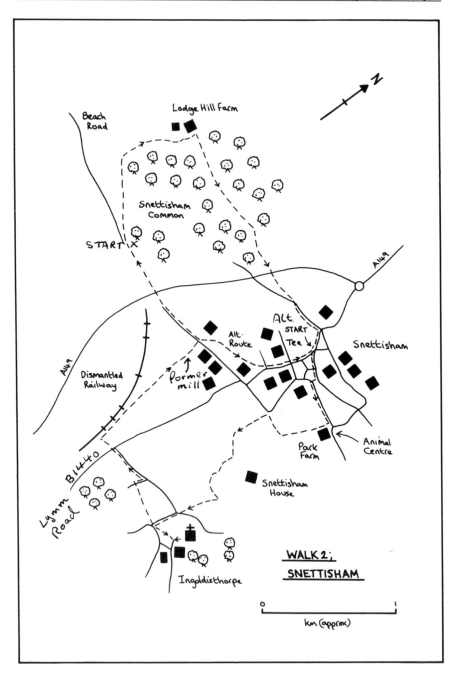

WALK 2;
SNETTISHAM

If not visiting the church, turn right immediately on reaching Shernborne Road, not along the road, but into a signposted public footpath to descend beside the hedge to an unsurfaced residential road. Turn right and then left in 40 metres along Hill Road. Reach the main road close to a pond; note the clock on the front elevation of a small terraced cottage.

Cross the road towards the Ingoldisthorpe village sign and continue along The Drift opposite. Turn right over a stile to take a good grass path beside Crossing Cottage. The next stile has an uncomfortably high step. The observant will already have noticed that we are now close beside a long disused railway line. After crossing the fields, pass the tiny former Snettisham Mill, with its waterwheel still partly visible through a window. Reach a minor residential road.

For the short walk turn right and then left in 30 metres to take a path through residential areas leading to the main road in a little under half a mile. Turn left to return to the parking area by the tea shop.

To complete the full walk, turn left along a street rich in old carstone and brick cottages to reach the main A149 by the former railway station area. Go across and follow a surfaced track (*or the road signposted to 'Snettisham Beach'*). In either case, pass the junction with Common Road and fork right in 20 metres into the car park.

3. Great Bircham

Length:	7¼ miles (shorter versions possible)
Summary:	A good country walk which includes a restored working windmill and the tiny village of Fring. The excellent paths include 2½ miles of the Peddars Way ancient trackway and about one mile in total on very quiet minor roads. No stiles or other impediments.
Car Parking:	To achieve the desirable objective of having refreshments part way round a walk, car parking in Fring would be recommended; however, only an odd roadside space will be found and the best solution is to park at Great Bircham Mill. Grid reference 760327.
Maps:	Ordnance Survey Explorer 23, Norfolk Coast West, 1:25,000 Ordnance Survey Landranger 132, North West Norfolk, 1:50,000.

Tea Shop

The visit to the mill complex is super – very peaceful and a definite East Anglian atmosphere with flat agricultural land and vast expanses of sky. Even if not visiting the windmill – it is quite a climb to the top! – do go into the bakery. The bread and cakes are made from flour ground on the premises and are for sale to take away; the products are of course also available in the cafe. It is counter service here with a small menu offering a sufficient choice for morning coffee, light lunches or afternoon tea. Plenty of tables indoors but very pleasant sheltered outdoor area to enjoy well-earned refreshments.

Hours: 10am to 5pm from Easter to 30th September every day except Mondays and Tuesdays. Tel. 01485 578393.

About the Area

Great Bircham is a pleasant village. The church is largely 15th century, with a fine 13th-century doorway. Inside is a 15th-century screen and a chancel restored in the 19th century; oak figures of men and women support the roof.

The feature which attracts most visitors to Great Bircham, however, is the beautifully restored working windmill, with the old tra-

Great Bircham windmill

ditional bakery at its foot. This complex also includes the recommended tea shop, cycle hire and a stable yard with attractions for young children.

Fring is a quiet hamlet with a rather plain little church. It lies on the fringe of the large scale lavender growing area, which has its headquarters at Caley Mill, Heacham. The bridge carries the road over the diminutive headwaters of the Heacham River as they leave the attractive pond near by. The Peddars Way is mentioned in the introduction to this book.

The Walk

From the mill car park return to the access lane and turn right. In less than a quarter of a mile join a minor road and turn left to walk between banks of cow parsley and forget-me-nots for about half a mile. Almost opposite a Water Authority pumping station turn right at a signpost to take a path rising gently by the side of a hedge, full of blossom in May.

Join a bridleway at the top of the hill and turn left. The path is along the edge of a field, ploughed rather close but still reasonable underfoot. Cross a field boundary, turn left then right to continue the same line, towards a lone farm building by the edge of woodland. This is prime Norfolk agricultural country, with light, sandy soil. Use by farm vehicles now ensures a better track for walking.

Pass along the edge of the woodland, Newton Plantation, mainly beech but with a few oaks. Turn left at a minor road to walk down to Fring, where the Heacham River is crossed by a little bridge by the outlet to the pond and a telephone box is the most significant feature.

Leave Fring uphill, after ignoring the road to Great Bircham and the road to the church. Keep left at a fork and, in less than half a mile and well before the top of the hill, turn left at a point where an unsurfaced track crosses the road. There is no signpost. We are now on the ancient Peddars Way which provides a fine tramp for more than 2½ miles, slightly up and down and not quite so straight as would be expected of a road used extensively by the Romans. The landscape embraces great fields of wheat and other crops, with the modest elevation resulting in fairly extensive views. The industrial cranes in the far distance are at the Bircham Newton Construction Industry

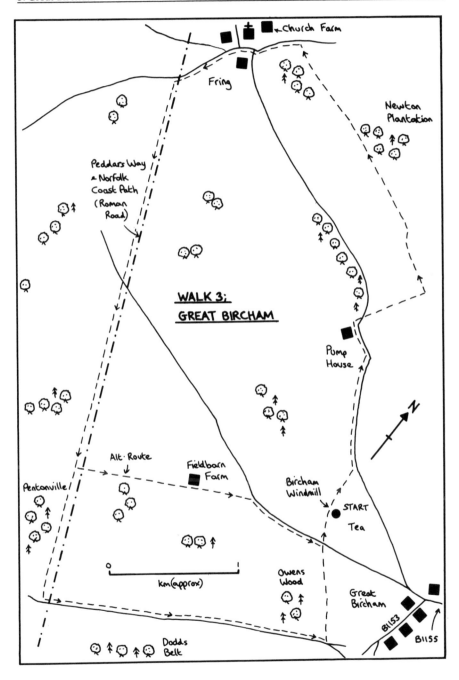

Church Farm

Fring

Newton Plantation

Peddars Way
& Norfolk Coast Path
(Roman Road)

WALK 3;
GREAT BIRCHAM

Pump House

N

Alt. Route

Fieldbarn Farm

Bircham Windmill

START

Tea

Pentonville

km (approx)

Owens Wood

Great Bircham

B1153

B1155

Dodds Belt

Training Centre, whilst the windmill at Great Bircham can be seen as progress along the Way is made.

Cross a minor road (*a left turn here provides the shortest way back to Great Bircham*). The Way continues as before, splendid underfoot; ignore a RUPP (*which passes Fieldbarn Farm as another short cut*) and continue for a further half mile, passing a wildlife conservation area with young conifers on the right

At a major junction of tracks turn left to follow another straight, level, green lane just like the Peddars Way. In about one mile pass Owens Wood on the left, quite a home for pheasants. Less than a quarter of a mile after the wood the first houses of Great Bircham can be glimpsed to the right.

Turn left along a very obvious farm track by the edge of a cultivated field, with an old hawthorn hedge on the right. Great Bircham Mill is soon in view ahead. Cross the public road and go down the mill access lane to return to the car park.

4. North Creake

Length:	4 miles
Summary:	A slightly up and down ramble through typical North Norfolk agricultural landscape, visiting the pleasant old village of North Creake and the ruins of Creake Abbey. Entirely first class underfoot and without stiles, a sociable walk where you can walk two or even three abreast for most of the way.
Car Parking:	Small parking area at Creake Abbey, reached by a right turn from the B1355 three quarters of a mile north of North Creake village. The right turn is the Abbey Farm access trackway. Grid reference 855395.
Maps:	Ordnance Survey Explorer 24, Norfolk Coast Central, 1:25,000 Ordnance Survey Landranger 132, North West Norfolk, 1:50,000.

Tea Shop

Apart from the delights of food and drink a visit to The Forge Tea Room should not be missed. There is claimed to have been a forge here for at least 850 years; Roy Masters is the blacksmith and his wife, Barbara, runs both the post office (her father was the postmaster for North Creake for twenty years) and the tea room. The furnishings in the tea room are fascinating. The light fittings are wrought iron, obviously made in the forge; there are two pianos and visitors (Grade IV or above!) are welcome to play. In one corner of the room is a very deep well. On cooler days, a wood stove burns. There is a very good choice on the menu with many items displayed on the counter. Service is very friendly in this pleasant cafe, with a welcoming atmosphere.

Open: 10am – 5pm every day from Easter to end of September. The remainder of the year open weekends and holiday periods including, surprisingly, Christmas Day, Boxing Day and New Year's Day. Tel. 01328 738910.

About the Area

Visitors to Norfolk might be forgiven for not knowing of North Creake or, indeed, its sister village, South Creake. Both straggle along the B1355, Fakenham to Burnham Market road. North Creake has plenty of good old cottages and a large, airy, church with a squat tower. Inside the church the high hammerbeam roof of the nave is adorned with 15th-century carved figures, all holding musical instruments, whilst the chancel roof has angels, some of them, unusually, bearded. There are two other rare features, firstly a revolving head on the lectern, with the Old Testament on one side and the New Testament on the other. The four gospel writers decorate the supporting column. Secondly, the large carved wooden cover for the font has a lower section which opens to reveal pictures and text.

Not on the line of the walk, but only a little more than one mile down the road, South Creake also has a fine church, notable for the survival of numerous richly decorative features inside, including a Madonna.

The ruins of Creake Abbey of St Mary are in the care of English Heritage. Founded by Augustinian canons, originally as a small hospital and almshouse for the poor, this was always an abbey of very modest wealth and influence. Following the receipt of endowments, it became a priory in the 12th century, being elevated to abbey status in 1231 by King Henry III. When the plague reached North Creake only the Abbot survived and the abbey was closed voluntarily in 1506, just a few years before King Henry VIII would have enforced dissolution.

The Walk

Leave the car park along the access trackway, back to the main B1355, passing North Creake Abbey Farm on the left. Cross straight over into a stony lane with hedges on either side, rising gently. Pass a substantial farm complex, well-screened by hedges. The countryside is pleasantly rolling. After a belt of coniferous woodland on the right, reach a fairly obvious junction, rather more than half a mile from leaving the road.

Turn left here to follow a farm track between a hawthorn hedge and a huge field, possibly with skylarks singing overhead. In half a mile a 'T' junction is reached; turn left here to proceed along another good track, soon beginning to descend, passing Mill Hill Plantation and then Long Plantation. North Creake church is visible across the fields to the right.

Join a public road by a children's playground, bearing left to walk

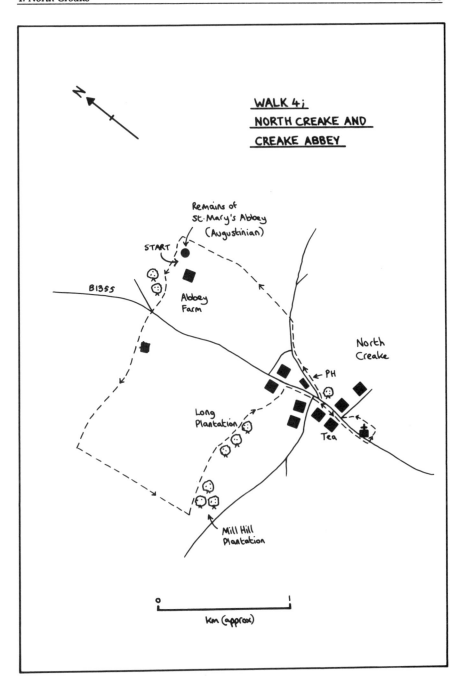

WALK 4i
NORTH CREAKE AND
CREAKE ABBEY

Creake Abbey

to the main road through the village. Turn right to walk to the tea shop in about a quarter of a mile.

After tea, *if the church is not to be visited, return along the village street to the cross roads and fork right.* However, it is recommended to turn right from the tea shop and to walk to the church in 150 metres. Leave the church by the south door, turning left. Turn left again behind the church to follow a mown track leading to a gate at the far side of the churchyard. Go through and follow a 'public footpath' sign, behind a house, down two steps and through a mini-woodland to rejoin the main road at a junction.

Continue along the road to the crossroads. Fork right into Wells Road and pass Glebe Farm. At a junction with a minor road there is an opportunity to avoid 200 metres of uphill road. Turn left at the junction then, in 40 metres, go through a gap in the hedge on the right. Follow the mown track rising close to the hedge on the right.

Leave the field at the top, turning left along a splendidly mown bridleway, a green lane with ample space for abundant growth of flowers on either side of the track. From the road this bridleway is an unmissable left turn close to the top of the hill. As the green lane ends, carry on along the edge of a field to join a rough roadway near cottages and turn left to return to the car park.

5. Burnham Market

Length:	5¾ miles.
Summary:	A walk which visits no less than four of the Burnham group of villages, with the added attraction of a length of the Norfolk Coast Path alongside coastal marshes. Footpaths are generally good. There are two miles of unobjectionable road, mostly with light traffic; a footpath beside the A149 is used for a short distance. One stile and two low bankings to negotiate. A fair amount of rise and fall, including the residential road leaving Burnham Market.
Car Parking:	Informal parking for about 12 vehicles at the far end of Burnham Norton village street. Grid reference 828442.
Maps:	Ordnance Survey Explorer 24, Norfolk Coast Central, 1:50,000. Ordnance Survey Landranger 132, North West Norfolk, 1:50,000.

Tea Shop

We expected Burnham Market to have lots of tea rooms but could find only one. However, only one is needed and this one is splendid. The cakes are scrumptious; especially the smooth carrot cake topped with lime and cream cheese. Scones are served with butter and jam. Should you make a really early start and complete the walk by 11.30am you could be self-indulgent and order the Norfolk breakfast! For a lighter savoury healthy option try the home-made quiche with salad. There is an amazing list of coffees with good attempts to describe the flavours. Other drinks available include hot chocolate topped with whipped cream, elderflower pressé, and, of course, tea.

Open: 10.30am – 5pm every day but closed on Sundays. Winter hours should be checked by telephone. Tel. 01328 730300.

About the Area

The various Burnham villages are all historically related to the sea having, at various times, all been ports of one sort or another. Progressive silting has pushed the sea further and further away and

Burnham Market

only Burnham Overy Staithe can now be reached by water, even by the smallest craft.

Paramount amongst these villages is Burnham Market, almost a small town, well-equipped with a good range of shops, banks, inns and other refreshments surrounding a most attractive tree-girt elongated central green area with a mini stream. There are medieval churches at either end of the village.

In contrast, Burnham Norton and Burnham Overy Town are quite tiny places, the former sitting on the edge of the great marshes which separate it from the sea and the latter having a noticeably squat church with a dinky little bell housing on the tower. Burnham Norton also has a church, situated nearer to Burnham Market than to the village which it serves.

Burnham Overy Staithe (quay) is the detached part of Burnham Overy, still retaining a maritime atmosphere. It is a minor boating centre close to the head of Overy Creek. At suitable states of the tide there are boat excursions to Scolt Head Island, which is a large nature reserve, one of the most important of the string of reserves, famous for bird life, along this coast.

All the villages have attractive cottages and other buildings, with a wealth of flint, old brick and mellow tiling. Another Burnham, not on the line of this walk, is Burnham Thorpe, famous as the birthplace of Horatio (Lord) Nelson, the great hero of these parts – look at the names of some of the inns. The church at Burnham Thorpe has a bust of Nelson, a collection of historic naval flags and other memorabilia.

The Walk

Start along the path which leaves the far end of the car park, passing a large cottage with a wealth of variety in the structure of its front elevation, reaching a signpost in about 50 metres. Turn right here for 'Burnham Overy Staithe 1 mile', along a grassy track. Go through/over a gate/stile. On the left, a typical coastal marsh extends to the distant sea.

The path keeps to the top of a sea defence embankment, with sea birds and wild flowers including a fair amount of wild briar adding to the interest. Go through a small gate to reach a junction of paths. Here we join the Norfolk Coast Path, bearing right to follow 'Burnham Overy Staithe'. Through a gap in trees to the right, Burham Overy Mill (no public access) is visible.

Cross a bridge over the River Burn to a gate/stile and continue across a field to reach the main A149 road. Turn left along the roadside path, keeping to the field for as far as possible. The relatively short section of roadside pavement has the interest of some good flint houses and well-kept gardens.

Turn left at the first road junction to walk along the Burnham Overy Staithe quayside, a quietly attractive area, usually with some boating activity. The adjacent Burnham Overy Marsh is a part of Holkham National Nature Reserve. As the quayside road bends back towards the main road, carry straight on along a waymarked path going left to a kissing gate to continue along the top of a sea defence embankment – taking note of the exhortation to beware of unexploded bombs!. The path is superb, with creek and marsh on one side and reclaimed grazing land on the other.

At a junction of paths after a seat, turn right to go through a gate and follow a broad farm track for just over half a mile. There is one locked gate with a high-stepped stile, followed by an uphill lane.

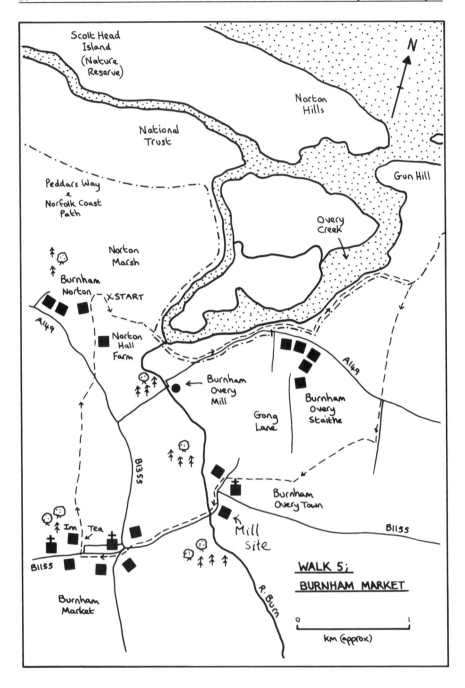

N

Scolt Head Island (Nature Reserve)

Norton Hills

National Trust

Gun Hill

Peddars Way & Norfolk Coast Path

Overy Creek

Norton Marsh

Burnham Norton

×START

A149

Norton Hall Farm

Burnham Overy Mill

Burnham Overy Staithe

A149

Gong Lane

B1355

Burnham Overy Town

Mill site

B1355

Inn   Tea

B1155

Burnham Market

R. Burn

WALK 5;

BURNHAM MARKET

0   1

km (approx)

The main road is reached at another locked gate, readily avoided to one side.

Cross the road and carry on uphill along a very minor road. In 300 metres turn right at an opening into fields; there is the post of a former sign on the left of the road. Walk along the edge of the field on the near side of the hedge for a little more than 100 metres, then go left over a low banking (sign) to continue diagonally across the corner of a field on a clear path. Go over another waymarked low banking to continue the same line across the next field to reach a junction of routes.

Bear slightly right into a waymarked green lane, heading for the now visible Burnham Overy church. Join a public road by a small scrapyard and turn left to walk through Burnham Overy 'town', a flattering title for a tiny village. At the junction with the B1155 road, the base of an ancient cross is evident. Keep right to walk towards Burnham Market, passing a large renovated water mill/windmill and crossing the River Burn.

On reaching the built-up area keep left towards Fakenham just before All Saints church, then turn right into Front Street in 50 metres, opposite the Lord Nelson Inn. The wide central area is soon reached. The tea shop is on the right.

From the tea shop turn right, then right again into Herrings Lane, by the side of an antiques gallery. The pleasant residential roadway rises past attractive, well-spaced, houses for nearly half a mile. Just over the top of the hill look for a track on the left in about 100 metres with a signpost 'Burnham Norton ½ mile' and a waymark. A rather narrow grass path stays close to the hedge along the margin of a large cultivated field, with fine views over Burnham Norton to the coast and a good-looking windmill to the right.

Join a farm track and bear right to the coast road. Cross over and continue along the Burnham Norton village street to the car park, passing a road junction and enjoying the attraction of numerous mellow buildings displaying the traditional Norfolk materials to good effect.

6. Brancaster

Length: 5¼ miles.

Summary: A walk which has the contrast of a length of the Norfolk Coast Path
                    across the back of the coastal marshes and a little of the Norfolk 'hill
                    country' at Barrow Common. Excellent footpaths and one and a half
                    miles along a very minor road. The coastal section is almost all on
                    board walk, with just one stile. The ascent to Barrow Common is very
                    gradual.

Car Parking: Layby on the A149 close to Burnham Deepdale church. Grid reference,
                    804443.

Maps: Ordnance Survey Explorer 23, Norfolk Coast West, 1:25,000 Ordnance
                    Survey Landranger 132, North West Norfolk, 1:50,000.

Tea Shop

The Old Maltings at Brancaster Staithe is the obvious venue for refreshments. This popular 'below ground' café has an ample choice of
sandwiches including crab, prawn, cheese and ham. Tea favourites
include buttered toast, tea cakes, homemade cakes, and pancakes
with syrup. There is a good choice of blends of tea and an excep-
tional number of coffees to choose from including Costa Rican, Ken-
yan, Colombian, and Viennese. Limited range of hot dishes such as
fish and chips – or try a special steak sandwich.
Open: 11am to 4 30pm every day but closed on Mondays. Hours
could vary and, especially out of main season, it would be advisable
to telephone first. Tel. 01485 210272.

About the Area

Brancaster, Brancaster Staithe and Burnham Deepdale are all quite
minor settlements, stretching for a total of about three miles along
the A149 coast road. Former little ports, they all now communicate
with the sea only via a series of winding channels through the
marshes. From Brancaster, a mile-long lane leads to the large, sandy,
beach through thickets of reeds. The sand dunes, shingle banks,
freshwater marshes and salt marshes of this area are very typical of

the North Norfolk coast as a whole. The old harbour at Brancaster Staithe is attractive, with a fair amount of pleasure boating activity and trips to Scolt Head Island, a large nature reserve, when the tide is right.

Between Brancaster and Brancaster Staithe the site of the former Roman fort of Branodunum can readily be visited.

Burnham Deepdale merges imperceptibly into Brancaster Staithe; the parish church has a fine round tower, probably of Saxon origin and an early Norman font.

Barrow Common is rather unusual for Norfolk – land rising to between 50 and 60 metres (about 180ft.) above sea level, largely gorse covered.

The Walk
Walk a short distance along the road towards Brancaster, passing a large petrol filling station and shop. Turn left and follow a minor road which rises very gently between hedges for 1½ miles. The broad verges are thick with cow parsley, studded with smaller, more subtle, flowers including plenty of clover. The wooded hill to the left is 'The Downs'; on the right is the attractive cluster of buildings of Valley Farm.

Burnham Deepdale church

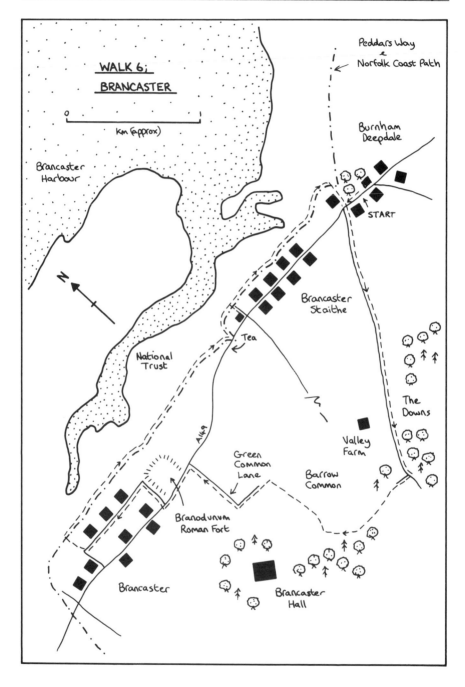

WALK 6;
BRANCASTER

0   Km (approx)

Brancaster
Harbour

Peddars Way
Norfolk Coast Path

Burnham
Deepdale

START

Brancaster
Staithe

Tea

National
Trust

The
Downs

A149

Green
Common
Lane

Valley
Farm

Barrow
Common

Branodunum
Roman Fort

Brancaster

Brancaster
Hall

Pass through a narrow belt of woodland, staying with the road as it bends sharply to the right. At a triangular road junction, with a waymark 20 metres in advance, turn right. Almost immediately, turn left at a signpost 'Branodunum 1 mile' to follow a narrow path, soon entering woodland. Initially a little lumpy underfoot, the surface of the path soon improves, reaching the open country of Barrow Common, with fine views to the sea from the top, where there is a main junction of paths.

Continue through a gate, now downhill, along a broad green lane. Go left at a junction, straight on at the next junction, then right in a further 100 metres. Reach the main road and turn left towards Brancaster; there is a decent roadside footpath. In less than 300 metres turn right into 'Stockings Lane leading to Cross Lane'. This little roadway soon turns sharp left.

Just past the bend is a gate on the right with an obvious footpath into the site of the Roman fort from which a connection to join the coast path may be made. This route does not however appear to be a right of way and cannot, therefore, be recommended by the authors.

To continue the full route, walk for nearly half a mile along the quiet little roadway through Brancaster. At the far end turn right into Marsh Drove by a 'public footpath' signpost. Go through the kissing gate at the far end and turn right to proceed along the Norfolk Coast Path (waymarked). In half a mile go over a stile on the right to visit Branodunun. A return to the coast path can be made at the far end of the field. Most of the coast path is on boardwalk, without which it would be quite impassable.

On reaching the buildings of Brancaster Staithe, turn right along a short road giving access to the main road. Turn right again to walk to the Maltings tea shop in 80 metres

Return to the coast path and turn right to continue. (signpost 'Burnham Deepdale ¾ mile). There is some mud underfoot at the back of the tidal creeks as a hotch potch of sheds, corrugated iron and boats, some of them disintegrating steadily, is reached. The path goes between tatty buildings, where there is a crude sign. Pass a small static caravan site; away to the left is the Scolt Head Nature Reserve, with a few low 'hills'.

Turn right, inland, at the back of a prominent creek, close to a flight of steps, and carry on along a broad lane leading to the main road. Turn left to return to the layby.

7. Wells-next-the-Sea

Length: 5¾ miles.

Summary: An attractive level circuit which includes a section of the Norfolk Coast
                  Path through a nature reserve, the grounds of Holkham Hall, the main
                  shopping street and the quayside at Wells. All tracks are first class and
                  there are no stiles or other impediments. There is even a small railway
                  which, in season, can be used to relieve the burden of the final mile (or
                  bribe the children) for those who so wish.

Car Parking: Large pay and display car park behind the beach reached along the
                  harbourside cul de sac road from Wells. Grid reference 914455.

Maps: Ordnance Survey Explorer 24, Norfolk Coast Central, 1:25,000
                  Ordnance Survey Landranger 132, North West Norfolk, 1:50,000

Tea Shop

The Ancient House Tea Room was an attractive discovery part way
round a most enjoyable walk – the perfect combination. The café is
pleasing with Windsor style furniture, good lighting, and divided
into small areas. Good choice of food and drink to suit all appetites
and a separate menu for children. Try the Holkham ploughman's
platter, smoked salmon sandwiches, or the Cornish (yes in Norfolk!)
cream tea. Pleasant outdoor eating area.

Open: 10am – 5pm from Easter to the end of October. Tel. 01328
710783.

About the Area

Wells is an interesting and not unattractive mixture, an old port still
functioning to some degree, overlaid by the manifestations of a minor seaside holiday town. The main shopping street is largely traffic
free, with a good selection of small, individual, shops; there is also a
frequent street market. Some areas of the town have elegant buildings and there are plenty of inns and other places for refreshments.
The tiny Maritime Museum on the Quay is well worth a visit for its
lively display of the maritime history of the district. The Wells and

Wells-next-the-Sea

Walsingham Light Railway (for more details refer to walk no. 8, Little Walsingham and Great Snoring) has its northern terminus on the fringe of Wells.

Holkham Hall is a considerable stately home, seat of seven generations of the Earls of Leicester. The house is in the classic 18th-century Palladian style and is open to visitors, generally during the afternoon, throughout the season. Also available are nursery gardens, bygones museum, pottery shop and the Stables Restaurant. Even when the house and gardens are closed, generous public access on foot is allowed in the extensive deer park which surrounds the house. Tel. 01328 710227 for information.

The Wells Harbour Railway operates a useful and attractive service, largely steam powered, on a mile long narrow gauge line, from the harbour to the Pinewoods Caravan Site, close to the beach car park. Operational from Easter to the end of October, but in the early and late seasons at weekends only. There is a boating lake and other amusements close to the car park.

The Walk

Leave the car park by facing towards the sea and then turning left along a broad track between the car park and the sea, with woodland on the right. This is part of the Norfolk Coast Path. The route contin-

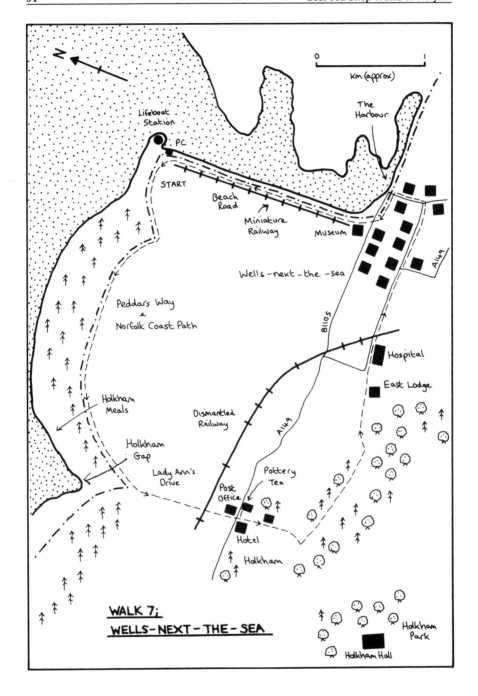

WALK 7;
WELLS-NEXT-THE-SEA

ues past a waymark and through a gate, then along the top edge of the boating lake. In 100 metres turn left at another gate to enter the Holkham National Nature Reserve.

Turn right at a 'T' junction, with a tidal warning notice, to continue along the fine track at the edge of the well-varied woodland of the nature reserve. The undergrowth includes a great deal of wild briar, bramble and, most attractive in May, festoons of honeysuckle. Smaller wild flowers are also plentiful and the bird population includes willow and sedge warblers

Go through a gap beside a gate and carry on to reach Holkham Gap in about 2 miles from the car park. A sharp turn to the right here gives access to the beach.

To continue the walk, go left through the large car parking area which lines both sides of Lady Ann's Drive and walk to the main road. Cross over and turn left for 40 metres to the Ancient House, where the tea rooms form part of a Holkham complex which includes gift shop and galleries.

Turn left on leaving the Ancient House, then left again by the Victoria Inn in 40 metres to walk along the Holkham street of estate properties. On reaching the formal entrance gateway to the estate grounds, go through and turn left immediately along a broad track through the woodland. Go through a gate with an unusual top and bottom fastening and continue to a junction of five tracks. Take the first track on the left, a surfaced roadway leading directly through Mousehill Plantation to East Lodge.

Pass the lodge and follow a broad, tree-lined avenue to the main road, A149, reached at a sharp bend. Walk along the roadside pavement, passing the local cottage hospital. Leave the main road as it bends to the right by the 'Wells-next-the-Sea' town sign and walk straight on. Pass a Congregational chapel and public conveniences on the left and then turn left into Staithe Street.

This is the town's main shopping street, a pleasing thoroughfare when vehicles are excluded. Browsing in the various bookshops may well prolong the duration of the walk! Pass the Tourist Information Centre to reach the Quay. Turn left along the quayside and then right to head for the Harbour Office and Maritime Museum. The station for the Wells Harbour Railway is over the road behind the museum. To finish the walk on foot, use either the path along the top of the embankment or the lower level surfaced pedestrian way, all the way back to the car park.

8. Little Walsingham and Great Snoring

Length:	5 miles
Summary:	A pleasantly easy walk from Little Walsingham to Great Snoring, returning by a different route. About 1¾ miles is along public roads but only the half mile or so in and adjacent to Little Walsingham carries a significant amount of traffic. Good footpaths generally, but one or two stiles to negotiate.
Car Parking:	Pay and display car park in Walsingham, at north end of village, well signposted. Grid reference 933369.
Maps:	Ordnance Survey Explorer 24, Norfolk Coast Central, 1:25,000
	Ordnance Survey Landranger 132, North West Norfolk, 1:50,000

Tea Shop

Walsingham Tea Rooms are found close to the post office, on the main street. Savouries offered include an all day breakfast, egg with chips, and bacon sandwiches. The usual items are available for tea, plus one or two that are less common such as cinnamon toast and crumpets. Most unusual of all is 'Bible Cake', very appropriate to Walsingham; the recipe can be purchased at the counter.

Hot Bovril, very welcome on a cold, wet, afternoon, and milk shakes supplement the more usual tea and coffee.

Open from 9.30am to 5pm daily except Fridays. Tel. 01328 820686

About the Area

Little Walsingham is a village (or small town?) of immense historic importance. Following the appearance of the Virgin Mary in 1261 in a dream to Richeldis, the local Lady of the Manor, a shrine was established, soon becoming second in importance only to Canterbury as a pilgrimage destination in Britain. The subsequent religious history has involved both Roman Catholics and, later, Anglicans through the centuries. On the southern fringe of Walsingham, close to

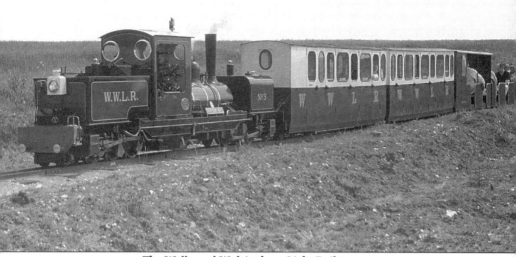

The Wells and Walsingham Light Railway

Houghton St Giles, the 14th-century slipper chapel, where medieval pilgrims would remove their shoes prior to starting the last mile of their walk to Walsingham, has been joined by the modern Roman Catholic National Shrine of our Lady.

Towards the northern end of the High Street the ruins of the abbey founded by Augustinian canons in 1151 are open to the public, with entry normally through the adjacent Tourist Information Centre. To the right, in Holt Road, a modern shrine (1931) was built by the Anglicans as a re-creation of 'England's Nazareth', as seen by Richeldis in her dream. The shrine has a setting in gardens, with accommodation for pilgrims adjacent. Abandoned in the time of King Henry VIII, pilgrimage to Walsingham was recommenced in 1897.

To complete the comprehensive religious presence in Walsingham, there is firstly a spacious Anglican parish church, mainly 15th century but with an older tower. Inside, the ancient font is the best of many features. Second is a Methodist chapel of 1794, claimed to be the only Georgian Methodist chapel in East Anglia still in use and, thirdly, there is the Russian Orthodox chapel of St Seraphim housed in the former railway station. The ruins of a friary founded in 1346 are incorporated into a private property with no public access.

Even without this overwhelming religious history and presence, Walsingham would still be a most attractive place to visit. Timber framed and Georgian buildings line the few streets, there is the old pump house, a curious beehive structure, whilst inns, tea rooms and the Shire Hall Museum behind the Tourist Information Centre also contribute.

At five miles in length, the Wells and Walsingham Light Railway claims to be the longest 10¼-inch gauge steam railway in the world. There are timetabled services to and from Wells next the Sea, a journey across farming countryside which is by no means as flat as might be expected. The principal locomotive is a fine and powerful 'Garrett' specially built for service on this line.

As a modest village, nearby Great Snoring can hardly compete in interest with Little Walsingham, but it does at least start with the advantage of an intriguing name, clearly displayed on the decorative village sign. Handsome terraces of flint and brick houses line the main street, and there is the large church of St Mary the Virgin, started in the 13th century but mainly of the 15th. The handsome rectory was built during the reign of King Henry VII, modified in the mid 19th century, and now serves as a guest house.

The Walk

Walk south along the main street towards Fakenham and stay on this road as it leaves the village, soon reaching an isolated farm lodge on the left. Turn left immediately to ascend an unsurfaced lane leading into woodland, soon becoming more open to the left. Continue along a roughly spaced avenue of mature oak trees to reach the top of the hill at a wide green lane, with more oaks on each side. At a fork go to the right; the lane narrows but the route is never in doubt, leading to the public road at Great Snoring.

Turn left ; there is a 'Thursford 2½ ' signpost at the junction, pass the former Rectory, and continue to the main road through the village. Go straight across the road, still following a 'Thursford' signpost. Pass Top Farm and, in about 100 metres, turn left along a slightly overgrown path at a yellow arrow waymark. Go round to the left over rough ground to pass behind the farm and then turn right to leave the farm complex, along a broad track fenced on both sides.

Go through/over a gate/stile and across a small field to a waymarked gate. The path now rises along the edge of a field. Turn

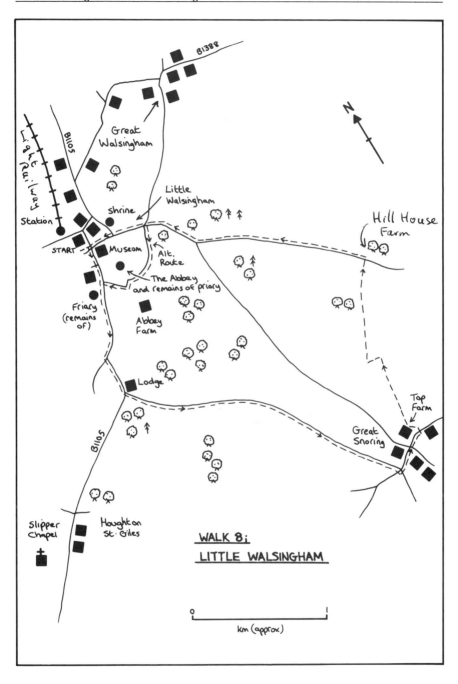

WALK 8;

LITTLE WALSINGHAM

0 _____ 1

km (approx.)

left, then right in 50 metres along the edge of a large cultivated field. At the next boundary turn left for a few metres then right along the far side of a hedge to reach the public road by Hill House Farm.

Turn left to follow the quiet road, soon descending. In about one mile join a more major road, by a World War II pill box, bearing right to walk to the Anglican Shrine. The road now rises into the centre of Little Walsingham for a direct return to the car park. *A pleasant short detour involves a left turn (well before the shrine) into a minor road leading to the parish church, continuing to the right and then turning right as the main street is reached.*

9. Blakeney and Cley-next-the-Sea

Length:	5½ miles.
Summary:	A level walk, very good underfoot, combining two outstanding coastal villages, both former ports. The inland section of the walk is mainly on roads, which are very minor indeed after the River Glaven has been crossed. The Norfolk Coast Path makes a delightful return round the edge of the Fresh Marshes.
Car Parking:	The Quay at Blakeney has a fair amount of informal parking together with a National Trust car park at the eastern end. Grid reference 028442.
Maps:	Ordnance Survey Explorer 24, Norfolk Coast Central, 1:25,000 Ordnance Survey Landranger 133, North East Norfolk, 1:50,000

Tea Shop

Whalebone House of Cley is a busy tea shop, so popular that at times a queue forms outside and you may be asked to share the big table – its all good fun and matey! Savoury platters are normally served between 11.30am and 2.30pm including 'The Cley Plate' – locally smoked mackerel with salad; 'The Norfolk Plate' – Norfolk ham with port terrine or 'The Whalebone Plate' – three British cheeses with apple, celery, and chutney. Old fashioned goodies offered include sardines on toast or Norfolk rarebit which is Welsh rarebit plus ham. The cream teas and home-made cakes are excellent.

Open: 11.30am – 6pm from beginning of April to the end of October every day except Mondays (open Bank Holiday Mondays and then closed on the Tuesday). From early November to end of March open on Fridays, Saturdays, and Sundays only from 11.30 – 5pm. Welcome to ring to check if in doubt. Tel. 01263 740336.

About the Area

A large village and former port, Blakeney is without doubt one of the nicest places on the Norfolk coast. Recession over the centuries has left contact with the sea, former lifeblood of the town, only via the Blakeney Channel. The extensive marshes, both salt and fresh, support abundant bird and plant life. The distant Blakeney Point is a well-known nature reserve, owned by the National Trust, renowned for seal viewing; local boatmen compete to provide trips to the Point at suitable states of the tide. Inland Blakeney has narrow streets with flower-girt courts and alleys separating the cottages, a mixture of flint and painted rendered walls. The church of St Nicholas, with 15th-century tower, stands massively on a low hilltop. Inside there is a lovely old hammerbeam roof with angels, and a soaring arch.

The former Guildhall, facing the Quay, is built of Flemish bricks. The undercroft has 14th-century brick vaulting.

Cley-next-the-Sea is a smaller settlement, once a busy port, and another place of great charm, with a dominant windmill facing the distant sea and many old flint buildings. This early 18th-century tower mill was used for corn grinding until 1918, being converted to residential use in 1938. Although the shops, inns and other commercial premises cling beside the main street (the A149) Cley straggles for well over half a mile inland, where the parish church is found. The tower is 13th century, but progressive rebuilding of the remainder of the structure continued until the 15th century. The result is a very fine church indeed with a great deal to repay careful examination.

The Walk

From the eastern end of Blakeney Quay walk inland, up High Street, passing two car parks which might be preferred to the quay, particularly at busy periods. Go straight across the A149, into Wiveton Road, passing the parish church with its massive tower. Follow the road, with bindweed and field edge poppies adding colour to the agricultural scene.

The Bell Inn is soon reached, facing Wiveton church across a green. Most of Wiveton village is to the left. Go straight on, following a 'Cley' signpost, downhill to a bridge over the River Glaven. Turn left at a crossroads with a 'Cley 1' signpost and continue along a minor road, passing reclaimed marshland on the left, to a large green with an inn. Behind is St Margaret's, the fine parish church of Cley.

Turn right, to rise along the path through the churchyard, then exit by a small gate, turning left along a surfaced lane leading into the main part of Cley, passing the village hall on the right. The road becomes a cul de sac; there is a pottery down a track on the left. Just

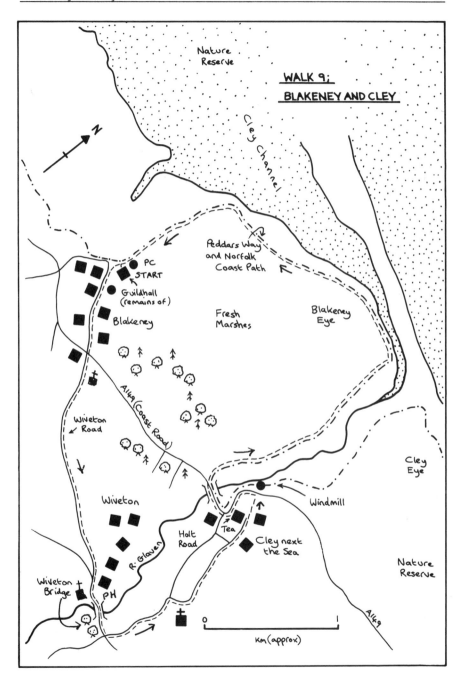

Nature
Reserve

WALK 9;
BLAKENEY AND CLEY

Cley Channel

N

Peddars Way
and Norfolk
Coast Path

PC
START

Guildhall
(remains of)

Blakeney

Fresh
Marshes

Blakeney
Eye

A149 (Coast Road)

Wiveton
Road

Wiveton

Cley
Eye

Windmill

Holt
Road

Tea

Cley next
the Sea

R. Glaven

Nature
Reserve

Wiveton
Bridge

PH

A149

0   1

Km (approx)

as further progress seems to be barred and the road loses its surface, go round to the left. In 20 metres follow a little sign on the right to 'Cley Mill and High Street', passing under an arch to reach the High Street.

To visit the windmill, which is occasionally open to the public, go straight across and take the unmade roadway.

Otherwise, turn left to follow the winding street, passing shops and an inn before reaching the tea shop on the left.

Continue along the street, going round a sharp right-hand bend at a junction. In a further 50 metres turn right up a few steps at a 'Blakeney 4km. 2½ miles. Norfolk Coast Path' sign. The route is now very simple to follow along coastal defence embankments. Cross the river on a footbridge, then shortly turn right towards the sea at a gate/stile. The view of the mill and village from the embankment is very fine.

Turn left at a junction, with a 'Protection of Sea Defences' notice. On reaching a wide creek with a shingle beach beyond, turn left to continue along the top of the embankment. As the path bends left to head for Blakeney, far away to the right is the hull of a beached ship. Keep left at a junction, pass another wreck and then a small waterfowl reserve to return to Blakeney Quay and car park.

10. Holt

Length:	5 miles.
Summary:	An easy level walk starting and finishing in the Holt Country Park, passing through the attractive country market town on the return section. No problems underfoot, but one stile.
Car Parking:	Holt Country Park visitor centre, accessed from B1149, south of the town. Grid reference 083374.
Maps:	Ordnance Survey Explorer 24, Norfolk Coast Central, 1:25,000. Ordnance Survey Landranger 133, North East Norfolk, 1:50,000.

Tea Shop

There are so many good tea rooms in Holt that choosing just one was difficult. However, The Coffee Pot tucked into one corner of Fish Hill, just off Market Place, was an enjoyable choice. Here we found cheerful decor with fabrics and crockery co-ordinated in blue and yellow. Our samples were carrot cake, scones, and a large pot of good quality leaf tea – all very good. Tempting specialities of the day are chalked-up on blackboards. Some tables out of doors.

Open: 9am – 4.30pm every day except Sunday but in the main season opens in the evenings and all day on Sundays. Tel. 01263 711800.

About the Area

One of the most attractive market (Friday) towns in Norfolk, Holt has a fine centre, bustling and full of individual shops, inns, tea shops and galleries, cheek by jowl in streets, alleys and yards. Rebuilding of much of the town after a great fire in 1708 has resulted in a predominantly Georgian ambience. Holt is widely known for Greshams, a public school founded in 1555 by Sir John Gresham, a former Lord Mayor of London.

Holt Country Park is a surviving portion of an old heath, with waymarked walks, car park and a small visitor centre which includes public conveniences.

The 'Holt Flyer'

The North Norfolk Railway, known as the 'Poppy Line' uses a restored portion of a closed railway line linking Holt and Sheringham with standard gauge timetabled trains, mainly steam-hauled. Out of high season, services are reduced, being restricted to school holidays and some weekends in the winter (no services in January). There is an intermediate station at Weybourne and the headquarters at Sheringham has static railway exhibits, shop and buffet. As the Holt terminus is approximately one mile from the town centre, connection is made by a horse-drawn bus – the 'Holt Flyer'

The Walk

At the car park, with your back to the main information board, follow a yellow waymark to take a narrow path opposite. After 20 metres turn left along a wider path, with waymarks including yellow. The path is first class, between dense woodland with rhododendron and bramble. Turn right at a junction to go slightly downhill, then left by the side of an attractive pond.

Bear left, uphill, at a junction, with another yellow waymark, soon reaching a tall observation tower. There is an information notice about 'Holt Lowes', an important wildlife area, managed by the Norfolk Wildlife Trust. Go straight on at this junction, with the Lowes on

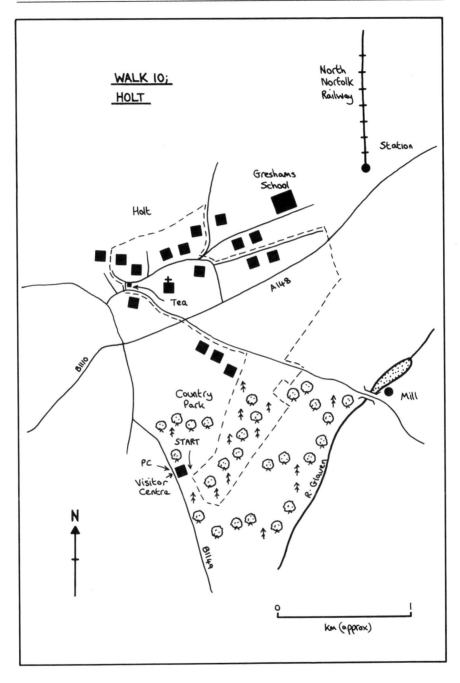

WALK 10;
HOLT

North Norfolk Railway

Station

Greshams School

Holt

A148

Billo

Tea

Country Park

START

PC

Visitor Centre

Mill

R. Glaven

B1149

N

0   1
Km (approx)

the right and woodland on the left. The waymarks are now red and blue. Pass a wooden sculpture on the left.

The track bears to the left; turn right in about 100 metres on to a narrow path, cross a boardwalk and turn right at a 'T' junction to go uphill. Go straight across at a junction, still uphill between conifers, to leave the Country Park over a stile on to a minor road.

Turn left to walk beside the road for less than 200 metres. Just after the speed restriction sign turn right to follow a signposted concrete surfaced private roadway leading to Heath Farm. The roadway has high hedges on each side, rich in bramble, enlivened by honeysuckle and bindweed. The farm has an impressive flint barn which appears to have included a house at the near end.

Turn left along a broad, stony, track leading to the main Holt to Cromer road. Go straight across to a signposted minor grass path, soon bearing left to a very minor road, Grove Lane. Continue for approximately half a mile, passing part of Greshams School. The road is lined by pleasant houses and gardens. At the far end, turn right at a 'T' junction to walk to Cromer Road. Turn right, then left in 40 metres into Kelling Road.

In about a quarter of a mile, 50 metres short of the speed de-restriction sign, turn left along a signposted footpath along the edge of a modern housing estate, with a tall hedge on the left. Go right then left through an opening in the hedge and continue along the edge of a cultivated field. Pass allotments before bearing left to a surfaced road and Holt town centre.

Go straight on along the road, passing trim flint cottages. This is Mill Street. On reaching a more major shopping street, go across into a bollarded alleyway to join the Market Place opposite the Feathers Hotel. Turn left and left again to the selected tea shop.

Continue by returning to the Market Place and turning left towards a monument, then forking right into Station Road. Just before reaching the bypass go left into a subway, then continue by the roadside for approximately a quarter of a mile. At the edge of the built-up area and just before a '30' sign, turn right at a public footpath sign into a broad track along the edge of the country park.

Go straight ahead at a wide gate with yellow waymark, then bear right at a red waymark on a post opposite a seat. Go straight on at the next junction (red waymark), now well inside the woodland. Ignore the next red waymark and go straight on; in 200 metres or so turn right to return to the car park and visitor centre.

11. Sheringham Park

Length:	3¾ miles. (An out-and-back extension to the coast adds 1¾ miles.)
Summary:	A great shortish walk within the National Trust owned Sheringham Park and Weybourne Heath, traversing a good deal of varied woodland enlivened in spring and early summer by a wonderful display of rhododendrons; there are also large open areas. Added interest is provided by a visit to the 'Gazebo', a high viewing tower, and to the 'Temple'. The North Norfolk Railway line runs close to Sheringham Park, with an accessible station at Weybourne. The route is more up and down than usual but, with one short exception, gradients are never very steep and the track surfaces and waymarking are excellent. The climb to the Gazebo is steep.
Car Parking:	National Trust car park accessed from A148/B1157 road junction, south west of Sheringham. Grid reference 140413.
Maps:	Ordnance Survey Explorer 25, Norfolk Coast East, 1:25,000 Ordnance Survey Landranger 133, North East Norfolk, 1:50,000.

Tea Shop

This is our 'cheat of the book' – we were keen to include this varied walk over National Trust land but the only provision made by the Trust for refreshments is a rather smart and discreet kiosk, with some picnic benches, just beside the main car park. Here one may purchase items such as hot and cold drinks, potato crisps, wrapped biscuits, and ice cream – enough to refresh, but not the 'tea shop experience'.

The alternative is to drive the short distance to either Baconsthorpe (walk no.14) or to Pretty Corner (walk no.12).

About the Area

Sheringham Hall and its immediate gardens are in private ownership, not open to the public. However, a huge tract of lovely countryside embracing Sheringham Park and Weybourne Heath is in National Trust ownership, with public access all the year round

The "Temple" at Sheringham Park

from dawn to dusk. There are several suggested routes, all differently waymarked, ranging from one mile to more than five miles in length, visiting such landmarks as the 'Gazebo', a tall viewing tower, and Thomas Upcher's (a former owner of the estate) 'Temple'. The rhododendron collection is magnificent.

The great landscape gardener Humphrey Repton (1752 – 1818) was greatly involved in the development of the park. After his initial survey of the park, he pronounced 'Sheringham possesses more natural beauty and local advantages than any place I have ever seen'. Prior to Repton, Cook Flower, an 18th-century owner, had planted the higher ground as woodland, leaving the valleys for the cultivation of crops; Repton built on this pre-existing basis.

The Trust has developed a visitor centre complex at the car park, including refreshments, information service, conveniences and occasional book and plant sales.

The nearby railway line is a great visitor attraction. (ref. walk no. 10, Holt, for more detail). A path to Weybourne station is a short diversion from the route set out below.

The Walk

Start along the 'red' trail, well signposted from the side of the car park. Don't be put off by the '5 miles' claim; that figure includes the extension to the coast given here as an optional extra. Fork left to follow stumps with red arrow waymarks at a junction in a few metres. The track among the trees is broad and well-trodden, soon reaching a steep little downhill section which could be slippery in wet weather.

The way becomes more open and there are attractive varieties of rhododendron. Note the occasional marker posts with red arrows before turning left at a major junction. Bluebells in spring and many other wild flowers are plentiful here and the bird population is abundant. At the next major junction turn right; opposite is a National Trust 'Weybourne Heath' sign. Pass a pond on the right to reach a very wide junction. Turn left here to cross Weybourne Heath, with bracken on the right for some distance. Keep right at a major fork, now going uphill, possibly accompanied by the occasional hoot from the nearby railway.

After another junction, with seat, go downhill to the edge of the woodland, above Weybourne station. The path follows the edge of the wood to the right, with views out to sea over Weybourne village. Look out for an apparently minor left fork leaving our broad forest roadway at a red arrow waymark and take this narrower path through the trees, soon leaving Weybourne Heath to re-enter Sheringham Park.

Go along the edge of a large field, uphill, to a meeting of routes by a gate.

If time or the weather are pressing, the diversion to the Gazebo can be omitted by carrying straight on here.

For the Gazebo and/or the coastal extension turn left then, in a little more than 100 metres, turn right, steeply uphill, aided by many steps. The Gazebo is a wooden tower about 12m. high, worth climbing for the extensive views. Return downhill and turn left.

To walk to the coast and back turn right after descending from the Gazebo.

Back at the gate, turn left to follow a well-worn track rising across a meadow, with Sheringham Hall to the left. Cross the entrance

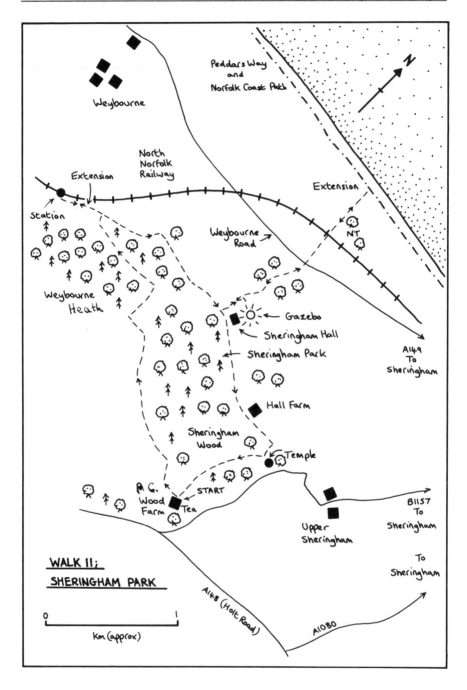

Weybourne

Peddars Way
and
Norfolk Coast Path

North
Norfolk
Railway

Extension

Station

Extension

NT

Weybourne
Road

Weybourne
Heath

Gazebo

Sheringham Hall

Sheringham Park

A149
To
Sheringham

Hall Farm

Sheringham
Wood

Temple

START

W.G.
Wood
Farm   Tea

Upper
Sheringham

B1157
To
Sheringham

To
Sheringham

WALK 11;
SHERINGHAM PARK

0   1

Km (approx)

A148 (Holt Road)

A1080

drive to the Hall, now walking along a surfaced track. Almost opposite Hall Farm, look for a little path with a red arrow and turn right along this grass path which rises to reach Thomas Upcher's 'Temple'.

Immediately after the Temple fork right over grass and descend to a gate. Go through to follow a rising track with woodland on the right. There are more superb rhododendrons before a broader, gravelled track is reached. Our red route crosses this track to head directly back to the car park, with a left turn as the outward route is re-joined.

A left turn at the gravelled drive uses the lower end of the 'Rhododendron Drive' to return to the car park.

```
┌─────────────────────────────────────────────────────────┐
│ ┌─────────────────────────────────────────────────────┐ │
│ │                                                     │ │
│ │            12. Pretty Corner and                    │ │
│ │            Beeston Priory                           │ │
│ │                                                     │ │
│ └─────────────────────────────────────────────────────┘ │
└─────────────────────────────────────────────────────────┘
```

Length: 4½ miles.

Summary: A mixture of attractive tracks down and up the hillside behind
                  Sheringham, visiting the ruins of Beeston Priory. The return part of the
                  route ascends through the wooded portion of the National Trust owned
                  Beeston Regis Heath. About 300 metres by the side of the main A148
                  road is included towards the end of the walk. Good paths with just a
                  little mud.

Car Parking: Good free car park at Pretty Corner, just off the A1082, near the
                  junction of that road with A148, well signposted. Grid reference
                  154413.

Maps: Ordnance Survey Explorer 25, Norfolk Coast East, 1:25,000. Ordnance
                  Survey Landranger 133, North East Norfolk, 1:50,000.

Tea Shop

Pretty Corner Tea Gardens – the reality is even prettier than the an-
ticipation – tea here should not be missed. The tea garden is, as a garden, absolutely beautiful. Furniture is of a very high standard with
sun umbrellas. Pleasant waitress service. The menu has everything
one might expect for an authentic tea garden tea – sandwiches, salads, scones, home-made cakes and ice cream dishes such as banana
split. Tea is served with milk or lemon; coffee, milk shakes, cold
drinks, are also available. There is also a well-furnished tea room
should the weather be too inclement for the sheltered garden.

Open: 10.30am – 5pm every day except Tuesdays, from April to October. Open weekends only in March. Tel. 01263 822766.

About the Area

The hillside rising behind Sheringham, West Runton and East
Runton to a long, high, ridge is justly well-known for its large areas
of woodland, predominantly open to the public, with car parking

and picnic areas contributing to the overall attraction to visitors. Pretty Corner is close to the highest ground in Norfolk, with a spot height of 98 metres, less than half a mile to the south east. The Norfolk Coast Path rises inland from Beeston Regis to cross the area, forming part of the route set out below.

Beeston Priory was always a small foundation, with just four Augustinian canons working within the local community as parish priests.

Nearby Sheringham is a traditional small seaside holiday town with a range of visitor facilities including tourist information and a museum. The North Norfolk Railway (see walk 10, Holt for more detail) has a terminus and its headquarters at Sheringham.

Beeston Priory

The Walk

From the north east corner of the car park a well-worn track leads into the woodland. There are so many tracks through Madis's Dale and Sheringham Wood that many people will find it difficult to keep to the following route directions exactly. If this happens don't worry – keep going downhill, with a bearing to the right (north east) – and you will end up close to the Water Company premises on the edge of Sheringham Common.

Here goes:- go right at a fork in a few metres, then straight on at the next fork for a few metres further, soon going downhill. Go left at the next fork towards a seat, now amongst some fine rhododendrons. Turn right at a more major track, briefly, and then left, temporarily uphill. Turn left at the next junction to resume the descent

Join another track and turn right, reaching a waymark, still downhill. Join a wider, major trail and turn left, passing a pond on the left. There is a bird watching hide here, but the key for access must be obtained. Keep left at a fork to join a major track by the edge of the built-up area, beside the Anglian Water Works.

Continue along a surfaced roadway; as the road bends to the left, go ahead along a footpath which runs parallel with the adjacent road. The distinct hill ahead reaches a surprising height of 63m.,very close to the coast. On the right is Sheringham Common.

Sixty metres before the gate which marks the end of this path, beside a sizeable oak tree, fork right to take a clear footpath, cross a footbridge over a tiny stream and go ahead to pass a pond with seats and waterfowl. Irises, gorse and humble buttercups make a colourful surround in spring. Continue ahead to reach a minor road, a cut off portion of the A149.

Turn right to the main road and then right again, crossing over to reach a waymarked bridleway in less than 100 metres. Turn left along a good path between hedges, soon becoming a broad grass sward by the ruins of Beeston Priory. After the priory pass a monastic fish pond then turn left along an unmade road. After reaching tarmac, turn right into Church Lane.

At the far end, by the railway embankment, turn right at a waymark to follow a path which stays beside the railway line for nearly half a mile. Turn right, beside a railway crossing, to follow a broad track back to the main road. Turn left, cross, and take a quiet roadway on the right. Join a waymarked stony track leading to Hall Farm and turn right. This track is part of the Norfolk Coast Path. Pass the farm and continue along a welcoming lane rising gently towards woodland, passing a touring caravan site.

Reach the lower edge of Beeston Regis Heath (National Trust) and go straight on at a 'Beeston Heath ¼ mile' sign. There are now almost as many tracks as in Sheringham Wood. The broad objective is to

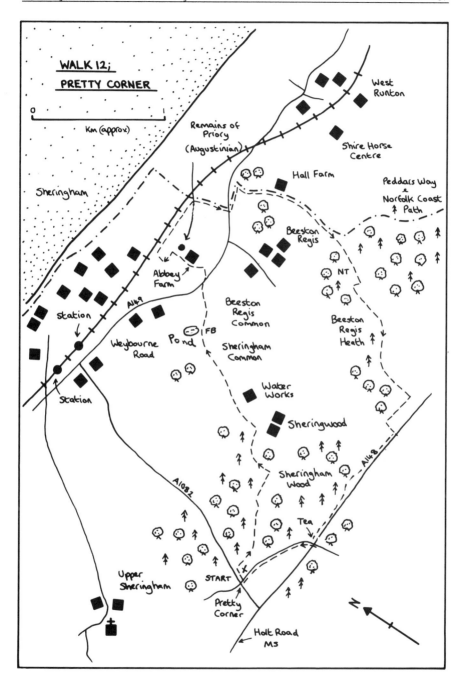

WALK 12;
PRETTY CORNER

0 _____ Km (approx)

Sheringham

Remains of Priory (Augustinian)

West Runton

Shire Horse Centre

Hall Farm

Peddars Way & Norfolk Coast Path

Beeston Regis

NT

Abbey Farm

A149

Station

Weybourne Road

Pond   FB

Beeston Regis Common

Sheringham Common

Beeston Regis Heath

Station

Water Works

Sheringwood

A1082

A148

Sheringham Wood

Upper Sheringham

START

Pretty Corner

Tea

Holt Road M5

N

keep west of North, so meeting the A148 as close to the tea shop as possible.

A narrow path, slightly muddy, rises through the woods. Go straight on at a junction where an N.T. waymark points to the right. The broader path rises steadily through mixed woodland with bracken and bramble undergrowth. A path comes in from the left, with an N.T. waymark; bear right here over level ground to a waymark on a tree 'Norfolk Heritage Coast' and turn left, still along a good trail, now with a fence a few metres to the right.

At the next multiple junction take a minor track, more or less straight on, still with the fence 20 metres to the right. The path curves strongly to the left; turn right at the next junction on quite a minor path. At a waymark on a stump go left, soon following the edge of the woodland with just a screen of trees between the path and a huge cultivated field.

As the main road is approached, turn right at a waymarked post, soon reaching a minor road. Turn left to walk to the main road. Turn right along the roadside verge; in about 200 metres fork right into a minor road which serves a civic amenities site. Rejoin the main road and walk 150 metres to a cross roads. Turn right to the tea shop.

After refreshments turn right to continue along the minor road to Pretty Corner car park, 250 metres distant.

13. Overstrand

Length:	3 miles.
Summary:	The length of the Paston Way along the coast towards Cromer is normally a beach walk; only at exceptionally high tides is it likely to be a paddle or necessitate an inland diversion. The return involves turning inland opposite the lighthouse and then using the roadside pavement on B1159 back to Overstrand.
Car Parking:	Pay and Display car park with public conveniences by the cliff top in Overstrand. Grid reference 247411. There is also limited street parking nearby.
Maps:	Ordnance Survey Explorer 25, Norfolk Coast East, 1:25,000. Ordnance Survey Landranger 133, North East Norfolk, 1:50,000.

Tea Shop

Although situated just above extensive golden sands, Cliff Top Café is a typical walkers' venue – not at all pretty but very functional. In addition to the usual choice of food, sandwiches and salads of lo-cally caught crab are sometimes available. Very pleasant to enjoy re-freshments at the outdoor tables and benches.

Open: 8am – 4pm every day from beginning of June to end of Sep-tember but closed on Tuesdays and Wednesdays in the other months. Also closed completely from just before Christmas to mid-February. Tel. 01263 579319.

About the Area

Overstrand is a gentle outlier from the hurly burly of Clacton; a place of leafy residences, inn, post office and a few shops, mostly sandwiched between B1159 and the cliff-edged sea. Inland is a con-tinuation of the ridge of largely wooded high ground which is such a feature of the Sheringham/Cromer area.

Structurally, the church of St Martin is a confusing mixture, basi-cally of the 15th century. However, the roof collapsed in the 18th century and the nave was partitioned, leaving the eastern end and

Overstrand

the chancel to decay. In 1859, a smaller church was built on the site. As this was outgrown, in 1911 the old church was enlarged and restored. Only the tower and the nave are now original.

The Paston Way is yet another of Norfolk's designated routes, taking its name from the Paston family, dominant landowners and merchants during the medieval and Tudor periods. Their fortunes, along with the title 'Earl of Yarmouth', were lost in the first half of the 18th century. The family has become immortalised by 'The Paston Letters', correspondence between members of the family during the period from 1422 to 1509 which have survived, providing a wonderful portrait of a colourful and dangerous age. The Way is a continuous route focusing on sixteen churches and their villages and towns in the north east of Norfolk. Overstrand and Cromer are included.

Nearby Cromer is still a popular 19th-century seaside holiday town, with a substantial pier. There is a railway service to Norwich along the 'Bittern Line'.

The Walk

From the car park, go down to the beach and turn left to walk over the sand towards distant Cromer pier. This is the recommended Paston Way route, although many walkers obviously prefer to use a well-defined path along the top of the low cliffs. Despite its popular-

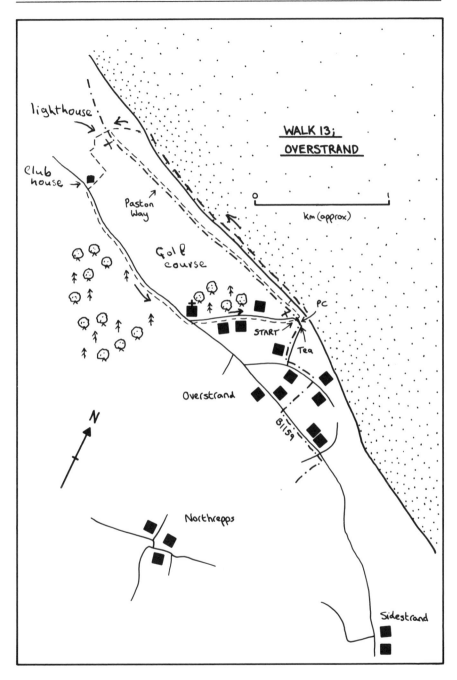

lighthouse

Club house →

Paston Way

Golf course

WALK 13;
OVERSTRAND

0 _____ 1
km (approx)

PC

START

Tea

Overstrand

B1159

N

Northrepps

Sidestrand

ity, this is, however, not a right of way and cannot, therefore, be recommended by the authors.

Opposite the inland lighthouse in a little over 1 mile, turn left to go up steps to a path leading to the lighthouse, then follow the roadway downhill, passing the golf clubhouse, to reach the main road beside Cromer Roman Catholic church.

Turn left along the roadside, heading for Overstrand church. Immediately past the church, turn left into a signposted public footpath between hedges. Join Paul's Lane and continue past well-kept houses and gardens towards the coast, reached beside the car park. Keep right to find the tea shop in a few metres.

Return by the same route to the car park.

14. Baconsthorpe

Length:	3¾ miles.
Summary:	A good short walk, generally through agricultural countryside, with the added interest of the ruins of a small castle and fortified manor house, and two villages. The walk is almost level, with good footpaths but there are several stiles to negotiate. Nearly one mile on minor roads.
Car Parking:	Substantial free car park at the castle, well signposted from Baconsthorpe village along a minor, then a farm access, road. Grid reference 121380.
Maps:	Ordnance Survey Explorer 25, Norfolk Coast East, 1:25,000. Ordnance Survey Landranger 133, North East Norfolk, 1:50,000.

Tea Shop

Margaret's at Chestnut Farmhouse had long been marked for a visit – it is highly recommended by the Tea Council. There are two tea rooms: The Harebell Parlour and the Strawberry Parlour – the decor throughout is absolutely delightful. There is also a very pleasant sunny tea garden. All the cakes and scones are made in the farmhouse kitchen and are truly delicious. There is a choice of plain, sultana, or cheese and walnut scones; toasted muffins; wonderful cakes, such as Victoria sponge, fruit cake, or lemon shortbread. Good choice of coffee and an almost formidable list of teas. For lunch the choice is from cooked meats, home-made flan, stuffed tomatoes with cabbage and apple salad, all served with bread baked on the premises and salad. Also available are open sandwiches.

Apart from the garden, this is not really a suitable venue for muddy boots and wet cagoules – so discretion should be used if eating indoors.

Open: 10.30am – 5pm from Good Friday to end of October. Closed Mondays except Bank Holidays. Winter opening hours are: 11am – 4pm weekends only and weather permitting, so it may be advisable to telephone first if in any doubt. Tel. 01263 577614.

About the Area

Agricultural, but not dull, countryside covers most of this part of Norfolk just a few miles inland from Sheringham. There is just enough rise and fall to avoid monotony. The ruins of the castle and the adjacent 15th-century fortified manor house stand more than half a mile across the fields to the north of Baconsthorpe village. The ruins are in the care of English Heritage and are open to the public daily from 1000 to 1600. Standing beside a substantial pond, they make an attractive grouping. Historical details are set out on an adjacent notice board.

Baconsthorpe village stretches, pleasantly enough, along a minor road, with church, post office/stores, inn and the rather special tea shop. The church has many monuments to the Heydon family, builders of the former manor. There is also a 15th-century carved screen, rescued from a village loft at Bessingham, now used to form the organ chamber.

Hempstead is a pretty village, with flint cottages and a part thatched church.

Hempstead Church

The Walk

Turn right out of the car park towards Hall Farm, reaching a post with waymarks. Turn left along a wide farm track, soon bending to the right along the edge of woodland. This is Hall Lane. At a junction turn right along a similar track, passing a seat as Beckett's Farm, trim and tidy, is approached.

At the farm follow the waymarks, left then right, to continue the same line as before, along a good field edge path which soon becomes a green lane between banks. A quarter of a mile after the farm turn left at a waymark; there has been an official footpath diversion here since the O.S. map was published.

Another field edge path beside a hawthorn hedge rises steadily to approach a very minor public road; the path, however, continues to the right, close to the road, for a further 200 metres. Join the road, turning right then, in 40 metres, turn left at a signposted footpath, a short length leading directly into the village of Hempstead.

Pass by the end of a row of houses to join a public road, Turn left to walk through the village. At the junction with Chapel Lane, the church is found on the right.

Turn left along Chapel Lane, turning right in a little more than 100 metres to take a grass path beside a hedge. Go under a natural arch, over a waymarked stile, cross a little meadow, rich in wild flowers, then over another waymarked stile and across an even smaller meadow. Pass a house to reach a public road at a gate/stile which appears to be permanently open.

Turn left to pass Tinker's Cottage and, after the road bends to the right, turn left into a farm track. In 10 metres turn right, up steps, to follow a signposted footpath, marked through the crop in a huge cultivated field. A water tower is in view, left ahead. Join a public road, turning left to walk towards Baconsthorpe.

Turn left at the second road junction, Long Lane, close to the water tower, and walk to the village post office at the junction with the main street. Turn right; the tea shop is about 200 metres further.

From the tea shop walk back towards the post office but turn right 30 metres before the road junction to go over a stile beside a farm gate and take a signposted clear path along the edge of a field, with a hedge on the left. Kink left then right (signpost), turn right at the next

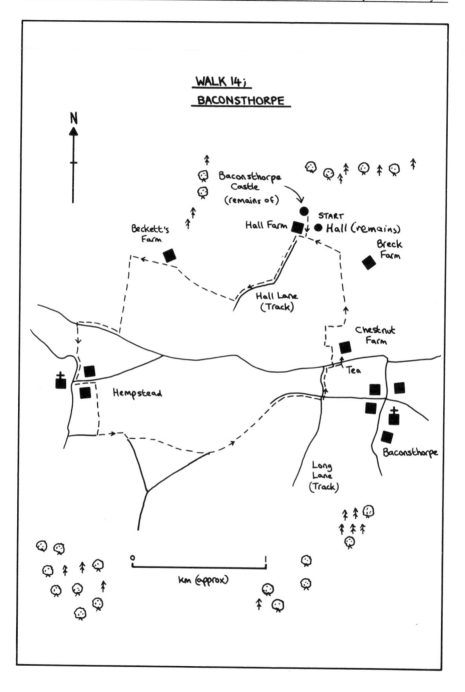

WALK 14;
BACONSTHORPE

N

Baconsthorpe
Castle
(remains of)

START
Hall (remains)

Hall Farm

Beckett's
Farm

Breck
Farm

Hall Lane
(Track)

Chestnut
Farm

Tea

Hempstead

Baconsthorpe

Long
Lane
(Track)

km (approx)

field boundary (signpost); the path hereabouts is ploughed rather close.

Go round a corner to a gate and rather overgrown stile with waymark. Breck Farm is to the right. The path continues much the same, with the castle ruin now in view ahead. Go over a stile and across a bridge to join a concrete roadway. Turn left to return to the car park.

15. Aldborough

Length: 5¼ miles.

Summary: A good mixture of footpaths and minor roads make a pleasant walk
                from the fine village of Aldborough to the Alby Craft Centre and back.
                Short lengths of path are slightly overgrown, as are one or two stiles,
                but overall, the route is easy. Two miles on very minor roads.

Car Parking: Plenty of informal car parking around the huge green at Aldborough.
                Grid reference 185343.

Maps: Ordnance Survey Explorer 25, Norfolk Coast East, 1:25,000. Ordnance
                Survey Landranger 133, North East Norfolk, 1:50,000.

Tea Shop

Alby Craft Centre at Erpingham is not to be hurried – the products
are truly crafted and many of the artists can be seen working.
Choosing just two from many, the embroidery shop combined with
a lace museum is packed with temptations to start you off on hob-
bies such as tapestry, whilst the wood turner can be seen making
beautiful wooden bowls and lamp bases. However, no doubt the tea
room will assume first priority. Here is pleasant counter service for
savouries, cakes, scones, drinks, and ice creams. Pots of tea served
under cosies – unusual these days. Morning coffee and light lunches
are also available. Attractive outdoor courtyard for sunny days. Noticeably reasonable prices.

Open: 10am – 5pm from mid March to mid December but closed on
Mondays except Bank Holidays. From mid January to mid March
open weekends only. Tel. 01263 768719

About the Area

Don't look for evidence of Benjamin Britten in Aldborough; his
home was some distance away at Aldeburgh on the Suffolk coast.
Norfolk's Aldborough is somewhat off the beaten track, a much qui-
eter place altogether. It is, though, a good village, with a spacious
central green, triangular in shape. Community Centre, inn, ho-
tel/restaurant, post office and a few shops are all, as they should be,

around this green. The large former water mill nearby has been converted into residential accommodation.

Alby consists of an inn, scattered houses and a handsome church with a 15th-century tower. Alby Crafts is a comprehensive visitor complex housed in converted former farm buildings, with more than a dozen individual craft workshops/museums. The four acre garden, with ponds and a collection of unusual shrubs and bulbs, is open to visitors at a modest charge. Tel. 01263 761590.

Aldborough – Alby Craft Centre

The Walk

Leave the village green at the southern extremity, by the children's play area. The adjacent village sign has an unusual thatched roof. Turn left immediately after passing a petrol filling station, at a 'public footpath' sign and a Weavers' Way waymark. A broad vehicular track leads to the former Aldborough mill. Bear left to follow the waymarks.

The path descends through woodland to a footbridge over a stream; cross and continue along an edge of field path. Join a minor road and turn right. Cross a more important road to take a footpath opposite – a narrow band across a cultivated field – initially heading for a concrete stump. After the stump, the path bends a little to the right to reach the next hedge, where there is an overgrown two-step ladder stile, down to the next field

This field is crossed on a similar path, again with an overgrown stile at the far end. Go over and turn left along a farm access drive, leading to Holl Road. Turn right to stay with this very minor road to a junction in about half a mile. Turn left here to pass a little duckpond with flotillas of mallard, then pass Thwaite Hall, an old building unbalanced by an extension at the right-hand end.

After a terrace of cottages the road bends to the left as the Weavers' Way joins us from the right. At a road junction go to the right; the Weavers' Way leaves us to the left after only about 50 metres of shared route. Pass another duck pond, with fine irises, on the right. As the road bends sharply right, keep straight ahead into a gravelled road serving several houses, signposted 'public bridleway'. The route becomes a narrow footpath, reaching the main road by the Alby Horseshoes Inn. Turn right to reach the entrance to Alby Crafts in 50 metres

From the craft centre return by the same route initially but, immediately after the first isolated dwelling on the right, turn right at a 'public footpath' sign to go up the bank and along a narrow grass path. You soon reach a huge cultivated field, where the route across is very clear. Alby church tower is visible in a gap in the trees far ahead.

At the far boundary of the field join a wide farm track by a waymark and bear right towards the church. There is a small modern windmill to the right. Cross the concrete forecourt of a large farm building and join a minor road close to the church. Turn left on the

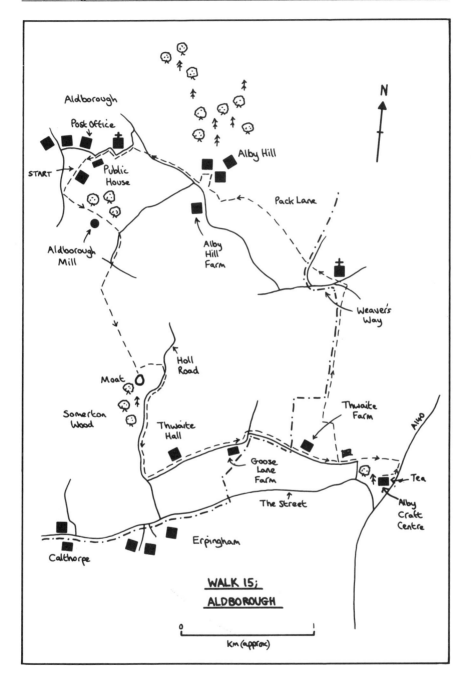

WALK 15;
ALDBOROUGH

0   1

Km (approx)

minor road, then cross a more important road. There is a waymark to the left of the church indicating a route through the churchyard. Follow this to the far corner where another waymark points the way along the edge of a field; the path is a little overgrown.

Reach a minor road and turn right; turn left in 50 metres at a 'public footpath' sign into a former green lane. This is Pack Lane, a pleasant old track, leading to the small settlement of Alby Hill, reached at the driveway to a house. Turn left, then left again in 40 metres along another driveway to walk to a minor road.

Turn right, pass a triangular road junction and Aldborough primary school. Cross a bridge over a stream then, in 50 metres go left over a good stile to cross a small meadow. Go over a similar stile on the far side, rejoin the road, and turn left to walk past the Primitive Methodist Centenary Chapel of 1907, the local surgery and the Community Centre to the village green.

16. Mannington Estate

Length: 3 miles.

Summary: A delightful short walk through the well-varied grounds of the estate surrounding Mannington Hall, with much of ecological interest, including a bird watching hide, a wet meadow close to the start and, later, Bridge Meadow, in course of restoration to its original state. Easy walking on good, waymarked, paths.

Car Parking: At the Mannington Hall visitor centre. Grid reference 143321.

Maps: Ordnance Survey Explorer 25, Norfolk Coast East, 1:25,000. Ordnance Survey Landranger 133, North East Norfolk, 1:50,000.

Tea Shop

We are assured that the small charge made for car parking allows entry to the grounds for those wishing to purchase refreshments at The Rose Tea Room. Self-service here – good selection of cakes including paradise cake and delicious but very rich chocolate shortbread; sandwiches, scones with butter and jam. Beverages include tea, coffee, iced tea, and other cold drinks. Prices are very reasonable. There is plenty of seating indoors but the patio is preferable – weather permitting.

Open: 12noon – 5pm on Sundays from early May to end of September and on Wednesdays, Thursdays, and Fridays from end of May to end of August. Tel. **01263 584175**.

About the Area

Mannington Hall is a moated stately home at the smaller end of the scale, owned by Lord and Lady Walpole, part of the Walpole family which includes Britain's first prime minister. The family also own the adjacent Wolterton Hall and estate. Neither house is normally open to the public but there is entry to the gardens (noted for the rose collection), shop and tea room at Mannington and to the parks of both houses. The Hall at Wolterton is open to the public on four days each year for guided tours only and to parties by arrangement. Both properties have conservation trail walks, including part of the walk set out below

The ruin of a claimed Saxon church is close to the gardens at Mannington, signposted but still requiring some determination to find. The park is open daily from dawn until dusk; the gardens, shop and tea shop are open from Spring to Autumn.

Mannington Hall

The Walk

Start from the front of the visitor centre, along an inviting grass track towards trees. There are waymarks on a post as the track bends to the left. In less then 100 metres turn right to cross a wet meadow on boardwalks. There are several routes across the ecologically rich meadow, the objective being to reach an area of rough grass and a little hide at the top end. From the hide waterfowl on an adjacent large pond may be observed.

After the hide turn right at a white waymark at the end of the meadow, along a wide grass track with several gates/stiles, bearing left across the front of Hall Farm Barn, built in the 1790s and re-

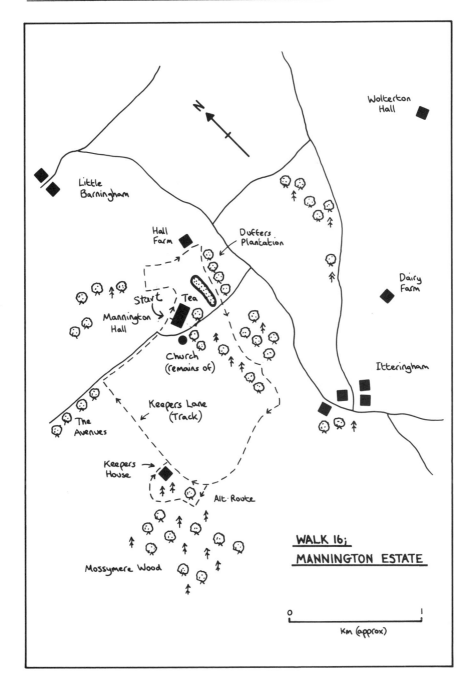

N

Wolterton
Hall

Little
Barningham

Hall
Farm

Duffers
Plantation

Dairy
Farm

Start   Tea

Mannington
Hall

Church
(remains of)

Itteringham

Keepers Lane
(Track)

The
Avenues

Keepers →
House

Alt. Route

Mossymere Wood

WALK 16;
MANNINGTON ESTATE

0   1

Km (approx)

stored about 20 years ago. Opposite the front of the barn turn sharp right, to walk along a field boundary, with Mannington Hall in view ahead.

A stile on the left in 40 metres gives an option to continue through Duffers (Dovehouse) Wood for the next part of the route.

Otherwise, continue along the edge of the meadow to reach a minor road. Turn right and then, in 50 metres, turn left at a waymarked iron gate. A lovely path now winds through largely coppiced woodland of hazel, alder and willow, known as 'The Cut'. This area is rich in small birds. Turn right at a clearing, go over a little footbridge and stile and follow the edge of Bridge Meadow, in process of being restored as a traditional meadow. As the path bends to the left, ignore a stile on the right.

Opposite a multi-waymarked post, turn right into a tunnel through the foliage and then go along an attractive green lane, rising gently between banks rich in bramble, Go straight on at a junction to reach the edge of Mossymere Wood.

A diversion through the wood along a waymarked path adds to the walk; it is essential to keep bearing right to return to the main route close to a dwelling).

Stay with the main track as it bends to the right to head north. Pass a dwelling on the left, then a part-ruinous farm building and continue to join the public road. Turn right to return to the Visitor Centre in approximately 400 metres.

17. Heydon

Length:	2¼ miles.
Summary:	A gentle stroll on level ground through a small village and part of the grounds of a privately owned historic house, returning along quiet roads. No stiles. Half of the distance is on minor public roads.
Car Parking:	By roadside in Heydon village. Heydon village is well off the beaten track, most readily found from the B1149, Norwich to Holt road. Take a minor road to the west about three miles south of Saxthorpe then turn right in just under two miles. Grid reference113273.
Maps:	Ordnance Survey Explorer 25, Norfolk Coast East, 1:25,000 Ordnance Survey Landranger 133, North East Norfolk, 1:50,000.

Tea Shop

Heydon Tea Room was our surprise find; in fact we arrived on opening day but believe that there had previously been a café here which had closed down some years ago. The new proprietor, Anita Pye, gives friendly and personal service, operating the necessarily small but very adequate menu. Here one can enjoy a cream tea, iced ginger cake, treacle tart, date slices, and other cakes. The sandwiches are excellent and a potato, cheese and onion pie with salad was also on offer. Mrs Pye deserves to succeed with this lovely café in this perfect village.

Open: 10am – 5pm but closed on Monday and Thursday afternoons. Hours could change and advisable to check before relying on this facility. Tel. 01263 587026 (home number).

About the Area

Heydon must be a strong candidate for the title of 'furthest off the beaten track village in Norfolk', accessed only by one cul de sac road, which is a turning off a very minor road, itself a connection from a fairly obscure 'B' road. Not surprisingly, Heydon is an estate village, totally owned by the family at the Hall, claimed to be one of very few such villages remaining in Britain.

Suffice it to say that the village is charming, well worth seeking out, with a large green, Victorian Jubilee well monument and a fine church, rebuilt in the Perpendicular style about 500 years ago. The interior has a box pew and a rood screen; of particular interest are the ancient wall paintings, whitewashed over centuries ago and revealed only when the wall was cleaned in 1970. Varied cottages flank the green; incredibly, there has been no new building in Heydon since the construction of the well in 1887; the village is much sought after as a setting for films and television productions.

The road passes through the village to enter the grounds of Heydon Hall. The Hall was built in 1582 by Henry Dynne; since 1640 it has been in the ownership of the same family – the Bulwers and Bulwer-Longs. Over the years, various additions were made, but by 1972 the house was in such disrepair that it had to be demolished or renovated. Most of the later additions were then taken down during comprehensive renovation, returning the building to its Elizabethan proportions. The Bulwer-Long family re-occupied the house in 1975. The gardens, which are occasionally open to the public, extend to about 15 acres. Visitors are welcome to walk in the park at all times.

The Walk

Walk past the gatehouse into the grounds of Heydon Hall; to see the Hall, bear right at once along a broad gravel track. Follow this track round, keeping left to pass the front of the Hall, then looping back to the original junction behind the gatehouse to complete a circuit.

Now turn right here along another wide track, passing a large meadow on the right before entering woodland. Pass a house tucked away among the trees on the right and then fork left at a grass track, which soon reaches the public road. Turn left to walk by the roadside to the junction with a more important road. Turn left and, in nearly half a mile, turn left again to return to the village.

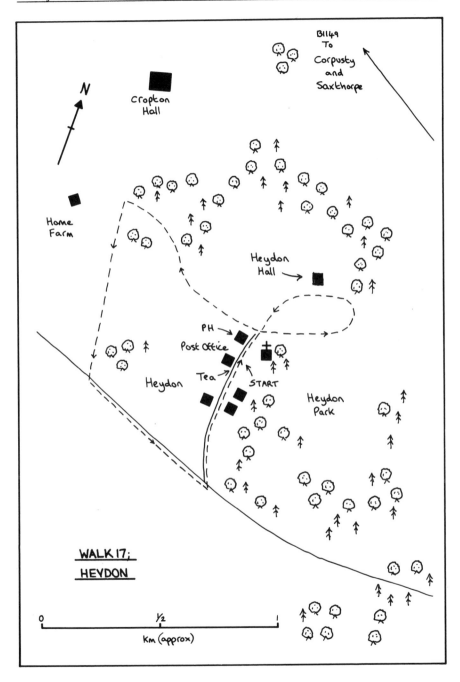

B1149
To
Corpusty
and
Saxthorpe

Cropton
Hall

N

Home
Farm

Heydon
Hall

PH
Post Office
Tea
Heydon
START

Heydon
Park

WALK 17;
HEYDON

0   ½   1
Km (approx)

Heydon Church

18. Reepham

Length:	8 miles.
Summary:	A circuit mainly on part of 'Marriot's Way', which is a large scale use of the trackbeds of two former railway lines, used also by cyclists and horse riders. A good connecting route is used to complete the circuit. The hub of this designated 'Way' is Reepham Station. The walk is very easy and comparatively level throughout; there are no stiles or difficult gates. The interest of the wildlife and the vegetation which has developed along the former railway line does much to offset any possible monotony.
Car Parking:	A start from a large free parking area at the former Whitwell Station is recommended, providing for refreshment at Reepham Station part way round the circuit. Whitwell Station is about one mile south of Reepham village centre, on a road which runs from Reepham to join A1067 near Sparham. Grid reference, 092216.
Maps:	Ordnance Survey Pathfinder 861, Aylsham and Foulsham, 1:25,000. Ordnance Survey Landranger 133, North East Norfolk, 1:50,000.

Tea Shop

Reepham Station is an interesting complex. The tea room is a popular spot for walkers, cyclists, and tourists. Food and drinks are served either out of doors at the front of the station building or in the attractive conservatory tea room on the platform. The floral crockery is attractive and the service pleasant. The menu includes sandwiches, filled baguettes, oven-baked potatoes, home baked sausage rolls, and salads. For tea try the scones, fairy cakes (not often found on menus these days) or Norfolk shortcakes. Filter coffee or tea available by the pot, mug, or cup. For something different the mulled drinks of apple or cranberry may appeal.

Open: 10am – 5pm every day except Christmas and New Year. Tel. 01603 871187.

Reepham Station

About the Area

Marriott's Way is named after William Marriott who was Chief Engineer and Manager of the comparatively small Midland and Great Northern railway system for no less than 41 years. He lived in the village of Melton Constable, an unlikely place to be the hub of the system, which then had engineering works which included a concrete factory, and all the other appurtenances of a railway depot. The present designated way, which extends to 21 miles, includes part of the M. & G.N. line from Kings Lynn to Fakenham and Norwich, combined with a section of the former Great Eastern Railway, an altogether larger company, which connected County School, near North Elmham, with Aylsham and Wroxham, a classic 'starting at nowhere and finishing at nowhere' line. From their construction in 1882/3 these lines crossed over one another at Themelthorpe, the tight curve which now connects them being constructed as late as1959, in order to allow concrete products from Lenwade to continue to be transported to Norwich after closure of other lines.

These lines were never very profitable as population was sparse and the varied freight, largely farm products, was insufficient. When the concrete production ceased, final closure followed in 1985. As is usual when railway lines close, a range of wildlife has colonised the former trackbed. Trees include oak, field maple, thorns, apple and the rarer spindle. Wild strawberry, haresfoot clover and primrose can also be found. Wetter sections support such species as marsh marigold, meadowsweet, reed and horsetail. Birds include jays, magpies and goldfinches.

Reepham is a pleasing little town/big village, with a fair range of shops and other commercial premises around its former Market Square, surrounded by mellow 18th-century buildings, some with a rather Flemish appearance. Very unusual is the inclusion of no less than three churches in one churchyard. One is nothing more than scant ruins, but the others, with adjoining chancels, are still in use.

The Walk

Go to the trackbed of the former railway line, behind the station building and turn right. Cross the road on a high bridge and continue. For some distance the track is on a low embankment and is obviously climbing as it bends to the left. The walking surface is first class. Cross the B1145 and then two minor roads on bridges. Brick Kiln Farm is down to the right.

The way bends continuously to the right as Themelthorpe is approached. Just short of Themelthorpe village a minor road, with gates on either side and a crossing keeper's cottage, is crossed. Here, before construction of the curve along which we are walking, the M.& G.N. went straight on towards Melton Constable.

Continue, soon passing the point at which the curve joins the former Great Eastern line, not easy to detect. Carry on along the Great Eastern, towards Reepham, more or less level and very straight. Butterflies and grey squirrels are fairly common on this section. Note a bridge wide enough to accommodate double track, surely over-optimistic! Cross a bridge over a stream. Forget me nots, dog daisies and red campion are noteworthy here, as are scampering rabbits.

Shut off steam and be ready to apply the brakes for Reepham Station and well-earned refreshments.

From the station walk along the old station approach to the public road. Turn right, then right again at once to follow Stony Lane. After a few modern houses this becomes a real lane. Reach a road with the railway line on a high bridge to the right. Turn left and then right in

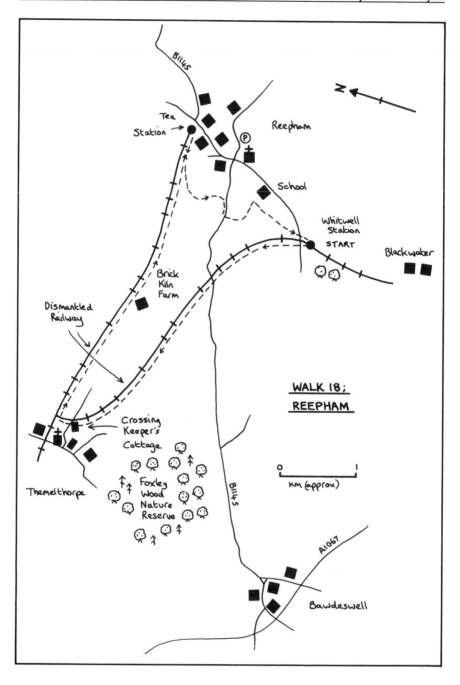

Z

B1145

Tea
Station
Reepham

P

School

Whitwell
Station
START
Blackwater

Brick
Kiln
Farm

Dismantled
Railway

WALK 18;
REEPHAM

Crossing
Keeper's
Cottage

0   1
Km (approx)

Themelthorpe

Foxley
Wood
Nature
Reserve

B1145

A1067

Bawdeswell

40m into a track with a 'public bridleway' sign and a Marriott's Way waymark.

This is a generally good track, with a few muddy patches. The route is never in doubt, following the edge of trees. On reaching a public road turn right for a little more than 100 metres, then turn left just after a rather dangerous bend. Follow a waymarked broad track, then turn left in front of a modern house. Turn right at a waymarked junction of paths, along the edge of a cultivated field, with a school playing field behind the hedge. On the right are some very old oak trees, including one of enormous girth. Continue to a minor road; turn left then right to return to the car park.

19. Blickling Hall

Length: 6 miles.

Summary: Not just a gentle perambulation round the grounds of a stately home, but a real country walk which includes some rise and fall and one section of rough footpath. Otherwise the tracks are good, the Blickling parkland is attractive and the roads which form part of the circuit are fine for walkers. Visits to the Hall and/or the gardens make a good combination with this walk. Several stiles, not all straightforward.

Car Parking: Free National Trust car park by the side of Park Farm, reached by the road which heads north from Aylsham, the Cromer road, turning left about three miles from Aylsham, then right in not much more than 100 metres. The site is on the left in a further three quarters of a mile. Grid reference 180296.

Maps: Ordnance Survey Explorer 25, Norfolk Coast East, 1:25,000. Ordnance Survey Landranger 133, North East Norfolk, 1:50,000.

Tea Shop

The chosen venue for tea at Blickling Hall is a very typical National Trust cafe. Boot friendly floor here, pleasing decor and friendly counter service. The varied menu offers light lunches such as soup, pasta dishes, and salads. The tea-time selection has scones and home-made cakes – the lazy daisy cake is unusual – a sponge mix with coconut and caramel topping. Menus are given on blackboards and the message chalked on one board said 'thank you for your visit we look forward to seeing you again' – a nice touch of encouragement to return.

Open: 10.30am – 5.30pm on Wednesdays to Sundays from 1st April (or Easter if earlier) to end of July and in September and October; open every day during August. From November to mid-December Thursdays to Sundays from 11am – 4pm.

Closed from mid-December to second week in January. From then until 31st March (or Easter) Saturdays and Sundays only from 11am – 4pm. Tel. 01263 738030.

Blickling Hall

About the Area

Blickling Hall is one of finest houses in East Anglia, truly a National Trust 'flagship'. The house dates from the early 17th-century and has fine collections of furniture, pictures and tapestries. Shop and restaurant/tea shop are accessible without paying for entrance to the Hall or gardens. The extensive gardens include mature yew hedges and topiary, a 'secret' garden, Victorian parterre garden and much more. Plants are sold. Perhaps of greater importance for our purpose, the estate as a whole extends to 4,777 acres, much of it parkland, with a large lake. This area is open to walkers all the year round, daily, from dawn until dusk.

The Walk

Go back to the access road and turn left. Pass through woodland and, about half a mile along the road, look carefully for a waymarked stile on the right, 100 metres or so before a house on the left. Go over, passing over swampy ground on a boardwalk. Cross a footbridge over a small stream and continue over grass. This is part of the Weavers' Way designated footpath.

Cross the River Burn on a footbridge, striding over rails at either end. In late spring there is a beautiful display of irises. The track follows the edge of woodland and there are even more irises, together with campion and the occasional squirrel. Keep to the right-hand boundary of a meadow and go over a stile on the right just before reaching a smallholding; keep to the left edge of a field to reach a waymarked signpost.

Join a green lane and carry on to a very minor public road at a bend. Turn left. The road bends to the left as Fring Wood Farm is passed, with a roadside cottage held together by tie rods. Continue along the road until the surface ends. At this point, follow a 'public footpath' sign along an unsurfaced roadway between cultivated fields, heading for a farm with woodland behind.

At White House Farm, turn left to follow a waymark. At a gate there is a choice of paths. Fork right to walk close to the hedge on the right; the path is barely visible over grass as it heads for a gate/stile. Continue across the next meadow, bearing right. The River Bure is close on the left, but only the occasional glimpse is possible. The route on this section is rough and not too easy to follow; keep close to the hedge on the right to reach a rather awkward stile. Cross two footbridges, then another stile with waymark.

Cross a muddy ditch and go on, to reach a junction of paths, with a stile immediately on the right. Turn left here to head for buildings, crossing two waymarked bridges over different parts of the River Bure, then a third bridge over a ditch to join a public road at a hamlet. Turn left to walk for half a mile on the road; as the road bends left, go straight ahead into a National Trust car park.

Go past a vehicular barrier and bear right to a gate. _A deviation to the left leads through Great Wood to the Blickling Mausoleum._ Go past the gate to follow an easy wide track along the edge of the woodland, with just one sharp little ascent. After the woodland, the way goes through fine parkland, heading for Blickling Hall. The building across the fields to the right is the 'Tower'.

On reaching a major junction of tracks bear right, go through gates and on to a roadway leading to the Hall, passing a tree with a circular seat and the Buckingham Arms inn on the right. Turn left into the main approach way; the tea shop/restaurant is on the right.

Start the return by the same route but, shortly after passing the Buckingham Arms, turn right at a 'Lakeside Walk' signpost, then follow 'lake and park' to go through a gate and take a grass path along the shore of the lake. At the far end of the lake bear right, join a more major track, then bear left back to the car park.

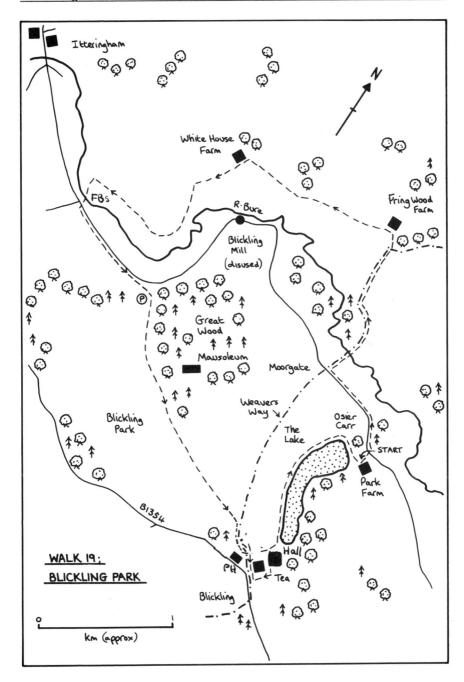

Itteringham

White House Farm

FBs

R. Bure

Blickling Mill (disused)

Fring Wood Farm

P

Great Wood

Mausoleum

Moorgate

Weavers Way

Blickling Park

The Lake

Osier Carr

START

Park Farm

B1354

WALK 19:
BLICKLING PARK

Hall

PH

Tea

Blickling

0   1

km (approx)

20. Coltishall and the Bure Valley

Length: 4¼ miles with return by train. (8 miles if walked both ways)

Summary: A rail and river mixture, with a walk along the valley of the River Bure
                   and a return ride on one of the splendid little trains (mainly steam
                   hauled) of the Bure Valley Railway. The paths are good and the route
                   is very level. One stile.

Car Parking: Bure Valley Walk car park at Buxton station, approached via a
                   residential road off the B1354 Aylsham to Coltishall road, 200 metres
                   west of Buxton church. Signpost at junction. Grid reference 232229.

Maps: Ordnance Survey Outdoor Leisure 40, The Broads, 1:25,000.
                   Ordnance Survey Landranger 133, North East Norfolk, 1:50,000

Tea Shop

Battees Restaurant and Tea Room is a welcome oasis in this
over-trafficked village. The menu is available at all times and includes pasta dishes, jacket potatoes, and hot crispy bacon sandwiches. There is a choice of cakes and sandwiches and drinks
offered include tea, coffee, cold drinks, and 'thick shakes' – Battees
version of milk shakes.

Open: Mondays, Wednesdays, Thursdays, Fridays from 11am –
4.30pm and on Sundays from 12pm – 4.30pm.

Also open on Friday and Saturday evenings, when booking is advisable. Opening hours could vary so check by telephone if in doubt.
Tel 01603 736626.

About the Area

Coltishall is a rather ordinary sort of village, its main claims to fame
being its position as head of navigation on the River Bure, a very important component of the Norfolk Broads cruising waterway system,
and its proximity to a famous Royal Air Force station. There are
moorings at Coltishall Common, a quarter of a mile downstream of
the village centre. The village always seems to have too many busy
roads for its size, all coming together at a filling station, perhaps a

rather symbolic heart. The church has Saxon masonry in the chancel walls although the building is generally of the 13th and 14th centuries, including a screen with delicate tracery. There are also some good old houses in the village

Coltishall does, however, have a station on the Bure Valley Railway. Using the track bed of a former Great Eastern Railway branch line (the same as at Reepham), which closed in 1988, the present 15 inch gauge railway was built in 1990 between Aylsham and Hoveton near Wroxham as a major visitor attraction. The line is nine miles long; at the Aylsham terminus the headquarters has a station which is quite sumptuous by narrow gauge standards, engineering workshop, shop and restaurant. Apart from during January and February, there is some service during each month; outside the holiday season this is restricted to school holidays. The attractive locomotives are well varied. Part of the overall tourist concept was the provision of a continuous lineside footpath, opened in 1991, with car parks and access points. Tel. 01263 733858.

Buxton Mill

Buxton is a relatively unpretentious village with an impressive former water mill of 1754, rebuilt after a fire in 1991, now in use as a restaurant. The parish church is of the 13th century.

The Walk

Leave Buxton station car park and walk along the trackside footpath for about 1 1/3 miles. The line stays close to the River Bure. Before Little Hautbois is reached, at a point where a public footpath crosses the line, turn right along that path to pass the lovely Little Hautbois Hall, built in 1607.

Turn right at a minor road and, just before reaching the river at Mayton Bridge, turn left at an informal space used for parking the occasional car. A waymarked permissive path starts at a stile here, over a plank bridge. Carry on along the riverbank, over grass to a waymarked bridge and then across another bridge.

The riverside path becomes steadily more attractive, lined with oak, willow, beech, elder and other trees, whilst coots and moorhens scuttle busily about their business. Stride over a large pipeline at waymarked steps. The river is now bending too and fro most attractively. Pass a deer enclosure and a section rich in irises and with willow branches trailing into the water. All in all, not a walk to be rushed.

Reach the fringe of Coltishall, go over a wooden footbridge and rise to the public road beside a bridge. Turn left; the tea shop is on the left in 70 metres.

Turn left out of the tea shop and bear left at the nearby road junction, heading for North Walsham. Keep right at the next junction, walking up Station Road, past the Railway Tavern. The station is on the left, just before the road rises to cross over the line. Either ride or walk from here back to Buxton.

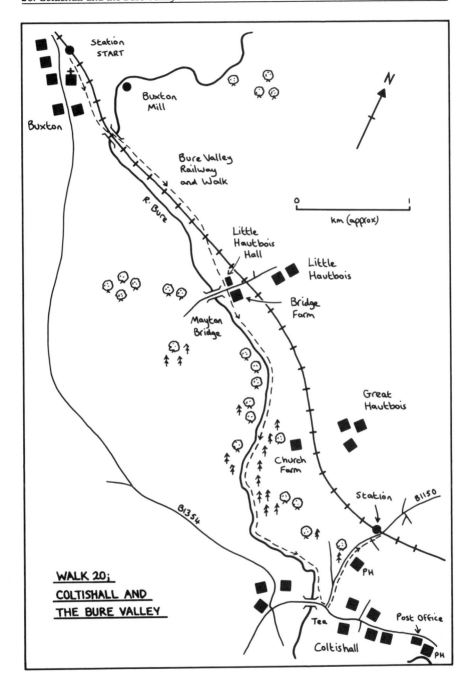

Station
START

Buxton

Buxton
Mill

Bure Valley
Railway
and Walk

R. Bure

N

km (approx)

Little
Hautbois
Hall

Little
Hautbois

Bridge
Farm

Mayton
Bridge

Great
Hautbois

Church
Farm

Station

B1150

B1354

PH

WALK 20;
COLTISHALL AND
THE BURE VALLEY

Tea

Coltishall

Post Office

PH

```
┌─────────────────────────────────────────────────────────┐
│                                                         │
│                    21. Ludham                           │
│                                                         │
└─────────────────────────────────────────────────────────┘
```

Length: 5½ miles.

Summary: A varied walk, with a section by the side of the marsh-fringed River Ant to the How Hill Broads Residential Study Centre and a straightforward path across fields followed by a minor road into Ludham. The return uses about a quarter of a mile of the A1062 then a track passing Ludham Hall before a little more of the A1062 completes the circuit. Good going underfoot and no stiles.

Car Parking: Close to Ludham Bridge, roadside laybys and informal area by the public conveniences. Grid reference 373171.

Maps: Ordnance Survey Outdoor Leisure 40, The Broads, 1:25,000.
Ordnance Survey Landranger 134, Norwich and the Broads, 1:50,000

Tea Shop

Alfresco Eating House is one of our favourite restaurants in Norfolk. David Mason describes himself as a poet and restaurateur. He seems to be ever present in a totally relaxed way, calmly producing food whilst talking to clients. Morning coffee is available from 10am. For lunch a variety of sandwiches are listed, whilst more substantial choices include ham and mushroom pasta, smoked salmon and cheese crepe, and other tempting dishes. Afternoon tea can be light or quite substantial – the brandy fruit cake garnished with mango, pineapple, and fromage frais is blissful! Coffee is first-class and only leaf tea is served – no tea bags here. Also worth trying are the home-made lemonade and Ranworth (local) pure apple juice. David is proud to say that all the food is prepared on the premises using only fresh ingredients. He also says that walkers are most welcome. There is a lovely sheltered courtyard at the rear for those preferring to eat outdoors.

Open: 10am – 5.30pm every day but closed all day on Mondays. Evening meals available but reservations are necessary. Closed for the first two weeks in November and from the end of January to mid-March. If in any doubt, please telephone. Tel. 01692 678384.

About the Area

Ludham is a pleasant village, with shops, inn, restaurant/tea shop and the mainly 15th-century church of St Catherine with its 14th-century chancel. The sturdy tower has a clock of 1762. The 1493 screen is decorated with twelve paintings, mainly of saints, and there is a great deal more of interest inside, including a fine hammerbeam roof and a well-carved 15th-century font.

The tea shop at Ludham

Landing stages and a boatyard at Womack Staithe, close to the village, are connected to the River Thurne by Womack Water.

At Ludham Bridge there is a cluster of shop/cafe, public conveniences, and boat moorings on the River Ant.

How Hill is an important residential study centre, set back a little way from the river, with a public picnic/recreation area occupying a large sloping field. By the riverside, tiny Toad Hole Cottage was an eel catcher's home, now open to the public to allow a glimpse of water based life and work in Victorian times. The cottage is open from May to October. An electric powered Edwardian style boat 'Electric Eel' operates 50 minute trips, nosing silently along the dykes and among the reed beds, providing first class nature viewing.

Ludham Hall, not open to the public, originated as a grange belonging to St Benet's Abbey, later becoming a bishop's palace. It was damaged by fire in 1611, then restored, with the addition of a little chapel, later put to use as a farm building

The Walk

At a 'public footpath' sign, turn right from the road to head north on a riverside path on the east side of the river, passing a long stretch of moorings. The remains of Neave's drainage mill are on the far side of the river in less than a mile. Ahead, a wind pump with sails and the large building at How Hill can both be seen.

Bend right, by an inlet from the river, and then left at a junction to return to the river bank. Pass Turf Fen drainage mill and reach the staithe (moorings) serving How Hill. The adjacent thatched boat house is the home of 'Electric Eel', which plies among the reed beds on the far side of the river. Water-based wild life is abundant here.

Turn right to find Toad Hole Cottage, now a mini museum of traditional Broads life.

Continue up the broad access track to How Hill. Pass the buildings and turn left at a very minor surfaced road, opposite the 'Mill House'. On reaching a few isolated houses turn right into a green lane, with a 'public footpath' fingerpost, slightly uphill. As the track bends to the left, turn right in a few metres along a narrow path carefully maintained across two cultivated fields, heading almost towards the distant tower of Ludham church.

Join a grass track on the far side of a hedge and turn right. In 50 metres, turn left at a waymark, along a field edge path. Cross a minor

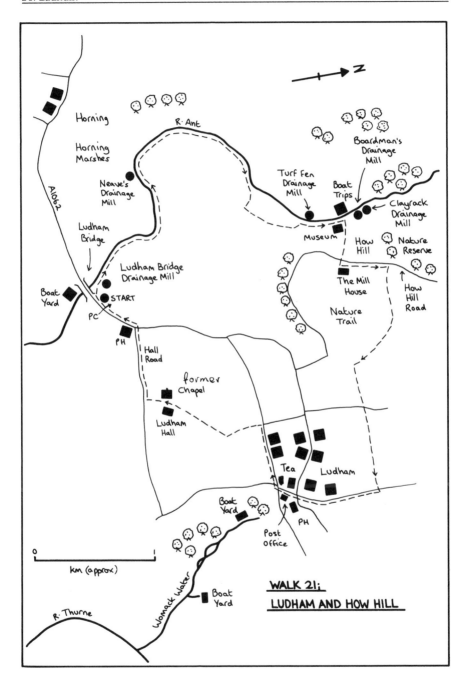

WALK 21;
LUDHAM AND HOW HILL

road and continue between cultivated fields, now with young oaks beside the path.

Reach a public road and turn right along the roadside path towards Ludham. At the cross roads in the middle of the village turn right; the Alfresco coffee/tea room is immediately on the right, with the fine parish church of St Catherine opposite.

Carry on along the main road for about a quarter of a mile. At a crossroads by a filling station, turn left into Lovers' Lane. Approximately 100 metres after the lane loses its surface, turn right to take a rising path towards Ludham Hall. The former chapel has had a large door added at one end. Turn right at a surfaced road and walk to the main road. Turn left past the Dog Inn to return to Ludham Bridge in a quarter of a mile.

22. Potter Heigham

Length:	5½ miles.
Summary:	Another totally flat easy walk linking the various parts of Potter Heigham village with part of the Hickling Broad nature reserve. A section of the Weavers' Way is used for the return route. Good paths and tracks; very few stiles.
Car Parking:	Large scale car parking areas at the boating area close to Potter Heigham bridge. Grid reference, 419186.
Maps:	Ordnance Survey Outdoor Leisure 40, The Broads, 1:25,000. Ordnance Survey Landranger 134, Norwich and the Broads, 1:50,000.

Tea Shop

We had some difficulty finding a tea-shop in Potter Heigham. In fact there isn't one! However, Carmans Cafeteria at Lathams Bargain Stores was a good choice for refreshments. It is clean, smart, and prices are reasonable. Cakes, scones, and sandwiches are well displayed at the counter or just ask for the hot pasties, sausage rolls, or toasted sandwiches. Hot and cold drinks and ice creams are also available.

Open: 9.30am – 5pm – every day all the year. Tel. 01692 670080.

About the Area

Sited on the River Thurne, a tributary of the more major River Bure, Potter Heigham is one of the most popular places in Broadland, drawing visitors in crowds during the holiday season. There are all the usual facilities such as shops and refreshments, overlaying the fundamentally boating purpose of this part of the village. Major boatyards have day boats for hire in addition to fleets of holiday cruisers.

Potter Heigham bridge has long been notorious as a steely-nerved test for amateur boat skippers, creeping through with heads down and inches to spare, with unwary crew members in danger of being scraped from their deck top sunbathing.

Physically, Potter Heigham is in three distinct parts – the riverside boating and visitor area – a small older part, with inn, a half mile to the north west – a detached residential area, with the distant church, on the north east side of the busy A149. The church is mainly of the 14th and 15th centuries, but with a Norman round tower and a handsome belfry. Inside, the large clerestory windows are striking; there is also a good hammerbeam roof, restored medieval wall paintings, and a 15th-century brick font among the attractions.

The Walk

From the car parking areas walk towards the bridge; turn left along a man-made track with a 'public footpath' signpost, parallel with the river. Go under the bypass road bridge and continue behind a long line of riverside bungalows, numbering to more than 100, which seem to go on for ever before a 'country' path is reached.

Turn left then right to a waymarked footbridge and the remains of a windmill, under restoration. Pass a pumping station and a few more waterside holiday homes then carry on along the river embankment. Bend round to the left at a junction of waterways, to head by the side of Candle Dyke towards Hickling Broad, with slightly rough grass underfoot, before reaching a sign 'National Nature Reserve – welcome to Hickling Broad – largest in the National Park'. The reserve is rich in plants and animals, including the rare swallow tail butterfly.

Go straight on towards woodland; the Weavers' Way soon joins us from the left. Go over a waymarked stile and into light woodland. A modern wind farm is visible to the right. Among the trees a very Broadland marsh habitat is apparent, but the path stays nicely elevated and dry underfoot. Although the open water to the right is seldom in view, the presence of boats is generally apparent.

Pass a jetty on the right, leave the woodland, and pass a bird watching hide which may contain a hornets' nest. The path bears to the left then to the right to reach more woodland and a waymarked stile. At a post with several waymarks turn left and cross a footbridge. The landscape change is considerable; it is now carr woodland at quite an advanced stage of progression.

Leave the National Nature Reserve at a stile, then turn right at a waymarked 'T' junction, soon bearing left along a broad agricultural track between cultivated fields. Potter Heigham church and dwell-

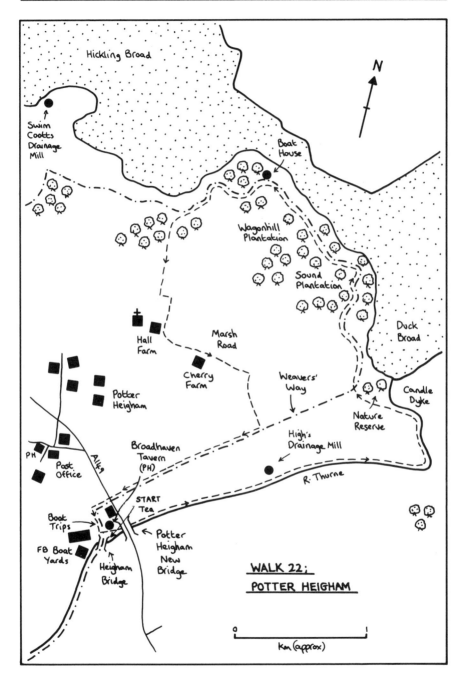

N

Hickling Broad

Swim
Cootts
Drainage
Mill

Boat
House

Wagonhill
Plantation

Sound
Plantation

Duck
Broad

Hall
Farm

Marsh
Road

Cherry
Farm

Weavers'
Way

Candle
Dyke

Nature
Reserve

Potter
Heigham

PH

Post
Office

Broadhaven
Tavern
(PH)

High's
Drainage Mill

A149

START
Tea

R. Thurne

Boat
Trips

FB Boat
Yards

Heigham
Bridge

Potter
Heigham
New
Bridge

WALK 22;

POTTER HEIGHAM

0   1

Km (approx)

ings are close. At the next 'T' junction, turn left along a well-marked field path. Turn right in 100 metres to proceed to a surfaced lane, turning left. This is Marsh Road.

Pass a farm and continue to the end of the lane, by an agricultural complex. Turn right here along a public bridleway. At a waymarked 'T' junction, join the Weavers' Way and turn right. The broad, very straight, track heads directly to the main A149 road.

Go across the road to a wide grass track, turning left at the next road in about 150 metres to walk to the tea rooms and the parking area.

Day boats at Potter Heigham

23. Horsey Mill

Length:	5 miles.
Summary:	A totally level walk without complications, on good tracks and footpaths, visiting the unpopulated coast and crossing typical Broadland countryside on the return section. Several stiles.
Car Parking:	National Trust car park at Horsey Mill, with public conveniences and a small shop close by. Grid reference, 456223.
Maps:	Ordnance Survey Outdoor Leisure 40, The Broads, 1:25,000. Ordnance Survey Landranger 134, Norwich and the Broads, 1:50,000.

Tea Shop

Poppylands – a lovely name for a tea shop in the part of Norfolk known for red poppies – is also a craft centre with pictures and hand-made articles for sale. This is a good place for tea part way round this well-varied walk. The home-made cakes and scones are excellent. Should you be passing at lunch time savoury dishes are always available. The poppy theme is followed through in the decor; the curtain fabric and table cloths are of a poppy design. The atmosphere of this rather special part of the county is well-described in a poem about Poppyland written in 1996 – just ask to see a copy.

Open: 11am – 4.30pm – every day except Monday. Open on Bank Holiday Mondays but then closed on the Tuesday. From the end of October to Easter, open weekends only. A telephone call is suggested if in doubt. Tel. 01493 393393.

About the Area

Of the many surviving windpumps in Norfolk, Horsey must rank amongst the best known and most visited. Now owned and operated by the National Trust, this former drainage mill of 1912 was struck by lightening in 1943 and put out of action. There is some original machinery, information boards and fine views from the top of the structure. The windpump is open to the public from late March to the end of September, daily from 1100 to 1700.

The coast visited on this walk demonstrates the efforts made to prevent the massive incursions of the sea which have, in the not too distant past, caused havoc in this low lying area. The usually deserted beach has literally miles of windswept sand.

Horsey itself is a tiny place with little more than a hall, one or two farms and a church. The latter has a Norman round tower with a 15th-century octagonal belfry.

Combining the coast with the inland dykes and Horsey Mere in one walk provides an unusual diversity of habitat and a consequent wide range of flora and fauna.

The Walk

Park at the National Trust car park beside Horsey Mill. Cross the road by the car park entrance, cross the ditch on a footbridge and go over a stile. There is no right of way but the Trust has created a permissive path, which is well-marked along the edge of a field, heading directly towards the coast.

Go over a waymarked stile to turn left beside a drainage ditch, soon reaching a surfaced road. Turn right. In 50 metres fork left by a house 'Crinkle Hill'. The road now loses its surface, becoming a bramble-banked lane crossing unproductive marshy land, heading for a gap in the dunes.

To see the beach and the sea go through the gap.

Otherwise, turn left; a good track stays parallel with the sea for about 1 mile, to reach an informal NT-owned car parking area. Turn left to follow the access lane back to the public road. Turn left to walk to the tea shop in 150 metres.

Return along the road, going round a left-hand bend, and then turn left in a further 100 metres at a 'public footpath' fingerpost to follow a narrow but clear path between fields. At the first hedge turn right at a junction, taking a path which leads to a few houses, Horsey Corner. Join a surfaced road, turn right, then left in less than 10 metres at a 'public footpath' fingerpost.

Continue over a bridge to a waymarked stile, then go left along a low embankment, soon bending to the right to head for a former windpump, the Brograve Drainage Mill. Just before the mill go over a waymaked stile and up the side of an embankment, then bear left by the side of Waxham New Cut, with abundant willow herb and tall

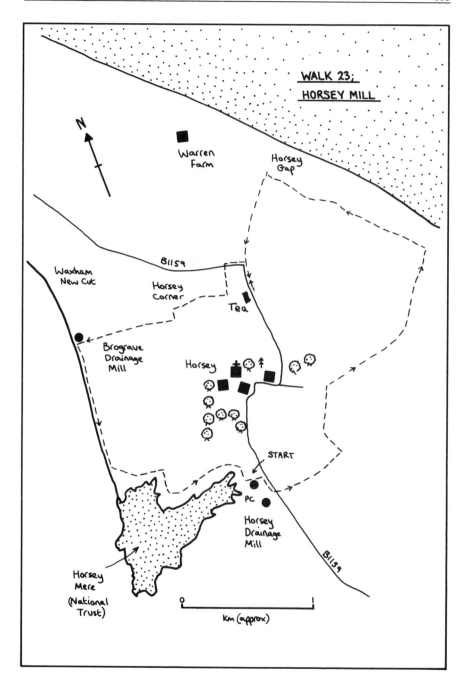

WALK 23;
HORSEY MILL

N

Warren
Farm

Horsey
Gap

B1159

Waxham
New Cut

Horsey
Corner

Tea

Brograve
Drainage
Mill

Horsey

START

PC

Horsey
Drainage
Mill

B1159

Horsey
Mere
(National
Trust)

0   1
Km (approx)

marsh grass on either side of the path. Part-way along this section, for environmental/ecological reasons, the path has been diverted a short distance away from the Cut; follow the white disc markers as advised.

Horsey Mill is soon in view. Go ever a stile and across an open meadow, heading for a white disc on the far side. Go over a stile and up a few steps to take the obvious route to the mill, passing boat moorings on the final section.

Horsey Mill

24. Stokesby

Length:	4¼ miles.
Summary:	A circuit intimately related to the River Bure, with its lively boating activity, in the Acle/Stokesby area. Much of the walk is along or close to the bank of the river or its associated drainage channel, Muck Fleet. The walk is level but much of the ground underfoot is lumpy grass, which many walkers might find to be uncomfortable. One stile (twice). Five hundred metres of minor road and 250 metres along the side of a main road.
Car Parking:	Excellent informal riverside car parking at Stokesby. Grid reference 431106.
Maps:	Ordnance Survey Outdoor Explorer 40, The Broads, 1:25,000. Ordnance Survey Landranger 134, Norwich and the Broads, 1:50,000.

Tea Shops

We were spoilt for choice in Stokesby and over-indulged by visiting two tea shops. Both are excellent; your decision may be based on the time of day and type of refreshment needed. **Riverside Tea Room and Village Stores** is just by the moorings and opens early, principally to serve breakfast to the cruiser crews, and continues serving to the end of the afternoon tea period. The tea room is a conservatory with pleasant decor and practical floor for those in walking gear. There is also an attractive terrace with tables and sun umbrellas. It is all very peaceful, and the cream tea is one of the best in Norfolk.

Open: 8.30am – 5pm. Every day from Easter to the end of September.

The alternative and equally enjoyable venue is **Candles Coffee Shop and Restaurant**. Here one can have anything from a coffee in the morning to a substantial meal in the evening or enjoy baguettes for lunch, or cakes, scones, and tea in the afternoon. A mouth-watering selection of cakes available included lemon, chocolate or coffee varieties. Pleasant service. Excellent outdoor seating area, and own moorings on the river.

Open: 10am – 9pm everyday but out of season open weekends only. Tel. 01493 750242.

About the Area

Stokesby is a charming little riverside community, with moorings, the Ferry Inn and general store/tea shop set around a green with children's play equipment. There is also a candle maker's workshop with refreshment facilities. The ferry which for many years provided the key to a shorter route to Acle and beyond has long been discontinued.

Acle Bridge is a well-known focus of Broadland boating activity, with boatyards, waterside inn, shop and public conveniences. Unfortunately, the A1064 main road crossing the bridge is often busy, a disruptive element in what would otherwise be a pleasant waterside area.

The small town of Acle, equipped with most types of shop and other facilities, is one mile down the road.

Wildlife in this predominantly wetland habitat includes marsh harriers, redshanks and lapwings.

The Walk

From the riverside, walk back to the road and turn left. Pass a tiny Methodist chapel and, a few metres before the candlemaker's premises, turn left at a 'public footpath' sign and a 'Broads Walk' waymark. The path passes behind the candlemaker. Go over a stile and proceed along a low embankment, with the River Bure close on the left. The grass path is well-defined but lumpy underfoot. Reach the Commission Drainage Mill which has a surviving brick tower, with a charming cottage and its garden beside.

In a short distance, turn right at a modern drainage pump to follow a concrete roadway beside Muck Fleet. At a junction with other similar roadways go straight on; there is a signpost as the track reverts to the rather rough grass encountered earlier, still following Muck Fleet. On reaching a very minor road turn left for 500 metres to walk to the main A1064. Turn left for 250 metres along a roadside path to reach Acle Bridge, with its various facilities.

The route back to Stokesby starts at a signpost reached immediately before a boatyard and before the actual bridge. Turn left, at first

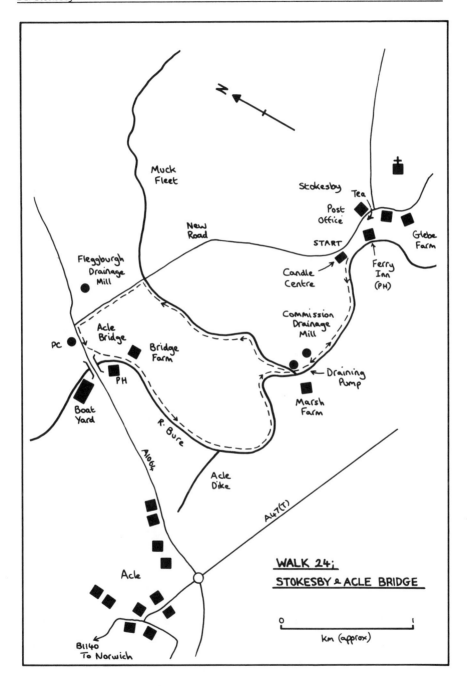

Muck Fleet

New Road

Stokesby

Tea

Post Office

START

Glebe Farm

Flegburgh Drainage Mill

Candle Centre

Ferry Inn (PH)

Commission Drainage Mill

Acle Bridge

PC

Bridge Farm

Draining Pump

PH

Marsh Farm

Boat Yard

R. Bure

A1064

Acle Dike

A47(T)

Acle

WALK 24;
STOKESBY & ACLE BRIDGE

B1140
To Norwich

0   1
Km (approx)

along a route carefully organised behind the boatyard, leading to the river bank. Turn left to walk along the well-cut grass. Pass Bridge Farm, striding over a low concrete barrier. The path continues as before, a typical top of embankment route on rather rough grass.

Across the water, the mouth of Acle Dike, which allows boats to reach the edge of the town, is passed, before arriving at Muck Fleet. Retrace the outward route from here to Stokesby.

Riverside cottage at Stokesby

25. Filby

Length:	2¾ miles.
Summary:	A wholly straightforward easy short walk, largely across agricultural land, linking Filby village with an unusual mill which is subject to reconstruction. The footpaths are good but there is some roadside walking. No stiles.
Car Parking:	Substantial informal parking area along the cul de sac road which leads to Filby church. Opposite the church hall. Grid reference 469134.
Maps:	Ordnance Survey Outdoor Leisure 40, The Broads, 1:25,000. Ordnance Survey Landranger 134, Norwich and the Broads, 1:50,000.

Tea Shop

Filby Bridge Restaurant is a purpose-built café with large windows giving views over Filby Broad – one of the Trinity Broads; the others are Rollesby and Ormsby.

Feeling energetic? Rowing boats can be hired from here. Morning coffee, lunches, afternoon teas and evening meals are all served but don't leave it too late for tea as closure is frequently at 3pm. There is a choice of cakes – but try the Norfolk shorties which are similar to scones – and the usual selection of drinks. Main meals available at reasonable prices.

Open: 10am – 3pm (sometimes later!) every day except Mondays. Tel. 01493 368142.

About the Area

Filby is a modest village immediately to the east of Filby Broad, largely strung along the A1064 and the Thrigby road to the south, where the village inn is found. The church has a 15th-century tower and 14th-century arcades. Inside is a font more than 700 years old and a six sided pulpit. Best is the chancel screen, with the 14th-century base having panels depicting saints.

Thrigby Post Mill is one of only two surviving post mills in Norfolk, built in the 1790s by the owner of nearby Thrigby Hall. By 1872

Ormsby Little Broad

death watch beetles had chewed their way through the timbers to such an extent that the mill was abandoned. Rebuilding started in 1982.

Thrigby Wild Life Park is less than one mile south of Filby village. The Park is a great visitor attraction, with a good collection of animals, well housed in the grounds of an old hall.

The Walk

Turn left, uphill, towards the church, passing a row of houses, and go through the churchyard, following a 'public footpath' signpost and a waymark. Immediately after passing the church go through a gap in a wall and turn left to a kissing gate. Turn right along a broad farm track.

Pass a large modern farm building, then a bridleway waymark on a post and continue along a path through a rising cultivated field. At the top of the field carry on past a post with waymark, now along the edge of a field. Turn right at a minor road to walk towards the post mill. The mill is behind a high hedge, best seen through a gate as the road bends to the left after Mill Cottages.

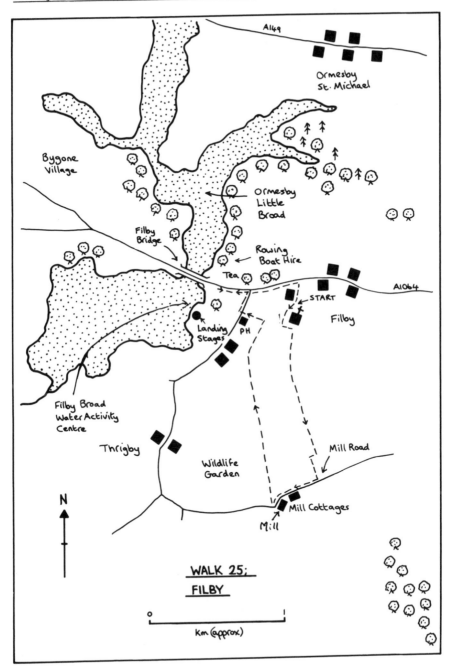

WALK 25:
FILBY

N

Km (approx)

Start back towards Filby at a roadside 'public footpath' signpost, crossing a huge cultivated field on a defined path, heading for Filby church. At the field boundary, go through the hedge at a signpost, turning right then left along a field edge. At a well-waymarked signpost keep straight on along a pleasant track with hedges on both sides.

At a 'T' junction turn left to reach Thrigby Road by the side of the Fox and Hounds Hotel. Turn right, pass the school, and reach the main road in 150 metres. Turn left to walk beside the road for nearly 300 metres to the tea shop.

Return along the roadside as far as the junction with Thrigby Road. There is now a choice:

Retrace the route past the inn, as far as the 'T' junction, then go straight ahead to the church and turn left to return to the car park.

Alternatively (and shorter), stay with the roadside pavement for a further 350 metres before turning right into the 'church' cul de sac.

26. Wymondham

Length:	3 miles in total (1½ miles each section)
Summary:	A most unusual offering here – two short walks, each of which is part of an environmental/conservation project. The two are not connected but are not too far apart, sharing the River Tiffey. Many walkers will be happy to explore both, including a visit to Wymondham Abbey, finishing at the splendid 'Brief Encounter'. The walking is entirely undemanding although there is the occasional stile and a few steps.
Car Parking:	a) Small public car park provided for 'River Walks', off Becketswell Road, between the Abbey and the railway level crossing. Grid reference, 105015.
	b) Small public car park at the Lizard, a minor roadway off Station Road, opposite the Station Approach. Grid reference, 116010.
Maps:	Ordnance Survey Pathfinder 902, Wymondham, 1:25,000. Ordnance Survey Landranger 144, Thetford and Diss, 1:50,000.

Tea Shop

A visit to the station is a unique experience, not to be missed. It is a combination of working railway station, railway museum, piano sales, and 'The Brief Encounter'. This themed restaurant has old railway carriage seats complete with luggage racks overhead. The walls are adorned with engine nameplates, insignia of railway companies, photographs, station lamps, and much more. Also displayed are nostalgic photographs and information about the famous romantic film 'Brief Encounter'. The corridor, piano room and the station master's parlour are filled with interesting railwayana. It is waitress service in the restaurant – choice of drinks from coffee to cola; for afternoon tea one can choose from crumpets, toasted tea cakes, banana bread, chocolate fudge cake and many other items. Between 12 noon and 2pm cooked meals such as sausage and mash, or chicken with rice are available; the daily specials are listed on the blackboard.

Open: 10am – 5pm every day all the year. Sundays open 11.30am – 5.30pm. Tel. 01953 606433.

About the Area

Full of interest for the visitor, Wymondham (pronounced 'Windam') is a fine little town. At its heart is an elaborate hexagonal Market Cross of 1617/8, repaired and restored in 1989, now housing the Tourist Information Centre. Markets are held on each Friday. Other attractive old buildings include the late 15th-century Green Dragon inn well-placed for the refreshment of those visiting the Abbey, from medieval pilgrims to today's tourists.

Outstanding is the Abbey church, founded in 1107. The church was intended to serve the Benedictine monks and the local parishioners but, as the respective rights were left unclear, there were many disputes between the parties, including the hanging and the ringing of the parish bells. Accordingly the people built the west tower in 1445 and the structure as a whole was shared between the two factions. At the 1538 Dissolution the Abbey church was granted to the people; the eastern end with the Monks' tower of 1390 was blocked up and allowed to decay. The consequent blank wall behind the altar was eventually covered by a great gilded screen to the memory of local men who perished in World War I.

The Bridewell, an ancient prison, was originally built in 1598, the present building on the site being a 'model' prison of 1785. It now accommodates the Wymondham Heritage Museum.

Very much a focal point of these walks, the railway station is quite unique. Firstly it is an operational station, with services on the line from Norwich to Ely and beyond. Secondly, the station buildings house a comprehensive railway museum and model collection. Thirdly, there is a gift shop and a piano showroom and, last but by no means least, there is the 'Brief Encounter', a café with the famous old film of the same name as its powerfully displayed theme.

Wymondham also has the terminus of the Mid Norfolk Railway, a restoration by a volunteer group of part of the former Great Eastern line linking Kings Lynn, Fakenham, East Dereham and Wymondham. At present limited services run from the headquarters at East Dereham to a small station close to Wymonham Abbey church and our first car park. The group intends to extend to North Elmham, County School and, eventually, Fakenham. Tel. 01362690633.

The market cross at Wymondham

The Walks

The Tiffey Valley Project

River valleys with grazing pastures are not very common in Norfolk. They offer a landscape very different from the usual intensively cultivated farmland. Much of the Tiffey Valley has been cultivated in the recent past, almost obliterating the outline of the original meadows. The present project has achieved the restoration of these meadows and future management will use traditional methods, resulting in a complex mixture of wildlife habitats. One stile.

Leave the car park by turning left along Becketswell Road, pass the Abbey church and bear left along Vicar Street. Charming old properties include the Vicarage with its mixture of flint and brick. Turn left again at the war memorial, passing the Methodist chapel before reaching the road junction at Town Green. Keep left along Cock Street, passing the half-timbered Oak House.

In a further 100 metres turn left into Froghall Lane (no sign), a wide, stony, driveway. In 40 metres go right at a fork and continue along a good wide track which becomes a footpath after passing a house on the left. Go over a waymarked stile and continue along a good grass path to reach a gate and a waymarked bridge over the river.

There is a choice here. A red waymark points to the right where, by crossing the adjacent railway line, an out and back extension of this delightful walk goes to Chapel Bridge, extending the overall distance by about half a mile.

For the basic circuit turn left; the excellent path now follows the river closely, with the track of the Mid Norfolk Railway close on the right. The well-varied flora includes lilies in the river bed. The car park is reached via a gate. To proceed to walk b), either drive via the town centre to Station Road and the Lizard or walk via Middleton Street, Damgate Street, White Horse Street and Cemetery Lane, passing the station and then crossing Station Road to the Lizard, a total distance of a little more than one mile.

The Lizard

This is a conservation area in the upper valley of the River Tiffey, including a small community of 17th-century cottages, homes for

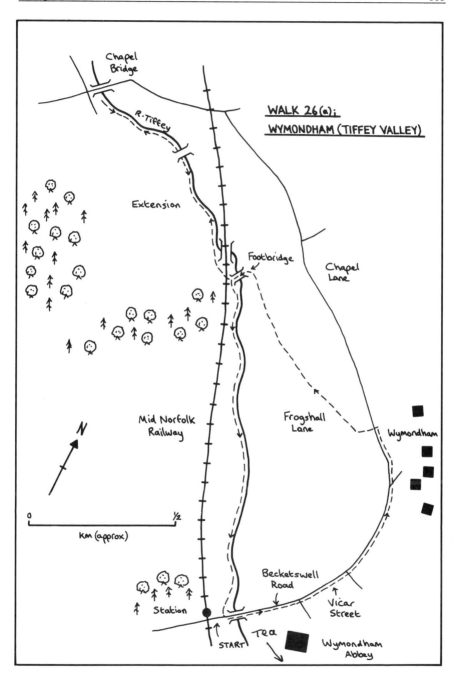

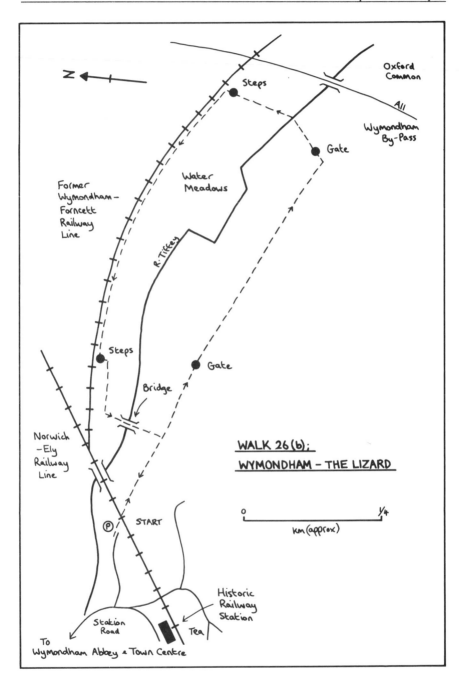

N ←

Oxford Common

A11

Wymondham By-Pass

Steps

Gate

Former Wymondham – Forncett Railway Line

Water Meadows

R. Tiffey

Steps

Gate

Bridge

Norwich – Ely Railway Line

WALK 26 (b);

WYMONDHAM – THE LIZARD

0 ————————— ¼

km (approx)

(P)   START

Historic Railway Station

Station Road

Tea

To Wymondham Abbey & Town Centre

weaving trade outworkers. Much of the land is in the care of a local charity. Two stiles.

From the Lizard car park turn left under the railway bridge and continue along a tarmac roadway, pass several houses, some of them the cottages referred to above. Go straight ahead at a little gate, provided with signs and a direction board. Follow a grass path through a natural meadow, rich in wild flowers. The tree-lined river is 40-50 metres to the left.

About 150 metres short of the busy by-pass, turn left at a fork, go through a waymarked gate, then cross a small bridge over the diminutive river. Continue over grazed grass to another waymarked gate. The towers of the Abbey church can be seen away to the left. Turn left immediately after the gate, over a slightly awkward stile and ascend the steps to the trackbed of the former Forncett branch railway line. Turn left along the top of the modest embankment.

Although a little overgrown in places, the path is generally good, with ox-eye daisies, wild briar, bramble and hawthorn in profusion, as are the rabbits and a variety of birds. A few metres before a wire fence, turn left down steps to leave the embankment. At the bottom turn right along a track reserved between fences, then turn left to a footbridge and head for an obvious stile. Cross a footbridge, ascend a few steps, with handrail, and rejoin the outward route, turning right to return to the car park.

---
27. Thetford Forest

Length: 5½ miles.

Summary: A good, generally level tramp along first class forest roads and paths, by no means all among the trees. Large areas are felled from time to time and the walk is more varied than might be expected. No stiles.

Car Parking: Spacious Forest Enterprises car park off the B1107, one mile north west of the roundabout where that road joins the Thetford by-pass. Grid reference 842841.

Maps: Ordnance Survey Pathfinder 943, Thetford, 1:25,000 Ordnance Survey Landranger 144, Thetford and Diss, 1:50,000.

Tea Shop

The café at the Forest Visitor Centre is a cheerful room with a high ceiling. As might be expected lots of timber has been used in the construction of the building and the tables and chairs are of sturdy wooden design; a wood stove burns on cooler days. The system is self-selection from the counter with orders taken for hot savouries such as toasted sandwiches or bacon baps – why not try the Hommity Pie? This is made with potato, cheese, herbs, and garlic. Good choice of cakes, scones, and drinks if visiting in the afternoon. Open: 10am – 5pm (or dusk if earlier) everyday from Easter to the end of the autumn half-term holiday. Remainder of the year weekends only. Tel. 01842 815434.

About the Area

Designated as a Forest Park in May 1990, Thetford Forest now attracts more than 1.5 million visitors each year. Claimed as Britain's largest lowland pine forest, Thetford is very much a patchwork which includes large areas of heathland and of broadleaved trees. As would be expected the forest has several species of deer, red squirrels and much other wildlife. Although it is very much a working, commercial, forest, producing 200,000 tonnes of timber each year on a sustainable basis, visitors, particularly walkers and cyclists, are very welcome.

The visitor centre at High Lodge is a comprehensive complex reached by Forest Drive, a toll road off the B1107. The Lodge has catering, picnic area, cycle hire, public conveniences, information and children's play area. It is the focal point of several of the colour waymarked trails which are such a feature of the forest as a whole.

Thetford Warren Lodge is the ruin of a building which was originally one of a group built around 1400 by the Prior of Thetford to house his warrener. The warrener had an important job, overseeing the production of rabbits for table from the warrens which covered the area. In the mid 19th century this area sent over 30,000 carcasses to market in London each year. The complex was largely destroyed by fire in 1935.

Thetford is a surprisingly ancient town, long ago the capital of East Anglia. There is a good deal for visitors to see, including the ruins of a great priory, the Ancient House Musem, and the Charles Burrell Museum. Part of the shopping centre is pedestrianised.

The Walk

Leave the car park, going slightly uphill on a sandy track, heading for the forest, between two old gate posts. The woodland closes in on either side and the ruin of the Lodge is passed. Pass a vehicular barrier and turn right; there are red, blue and yellow bands on a stump.

Pass through Rishbeth Wood, with pines, oak, beech and larch. Turn left at a 'T' junction, then right in 50 metres. Both junctions have marker posts; we are now on a route which is solely red, part of a waymarked trail based on Warren Lodge. Continue through more of Rishbeth Wood, this portion being fairly recently planted, along a broad, pleasant, grass track Go straight ahead at any junction.

Bend a little to the left, cross the vehicular Forest Drive and continue. In a further a quarter of a mile the red circuit turns left at a junction; keep straight on, still on a broad grass track, predominantly between pines. Turn left at a 'T' junction. On approaching Forest Drive again, turn sharp right before the Drive along another broad grass track. In a quarter of a mile turn left, then right in 20 metres to continue the previous line along a well-tended track. Join the orange trail which connects High Lodge with an observation hide and turn sharp left to follow this trail, crossing the Forest Drive on the way into the visitor centre.

Leaving the visitor centre for the return can be a little tricky as

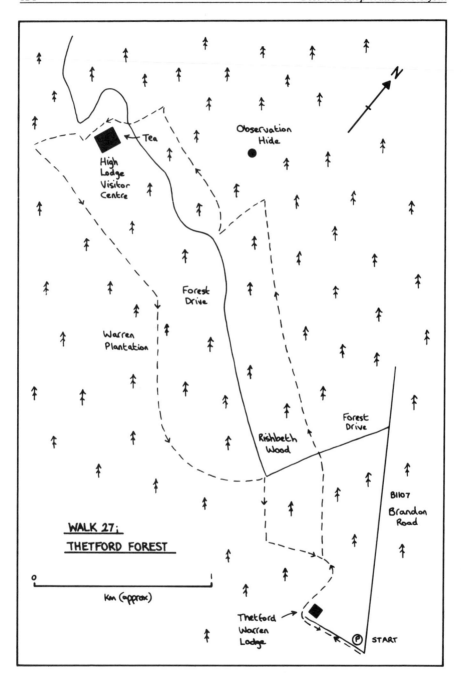

N

Observation
Hide

Tea

High
Lodge
Visitor
Centre

Forest
Drive

Warren
Plantation

Forest
Drive

Rishbeth
Wood

B1107
Brandon
Road

WALK 27:

THETFORD FOREST

0   1

Km (approx)

Thetford
Warren
Lodge

START

there are so many tracks waymarked for different purposes. The first half a mile or so uses part of a yellow-posted route. The safest way to find the start of this track is to walk away from the refreshment room and picnic area to a yellow capped post. Continue to the bottom right corner of the cleared area and go straight on, heading south, as the yellow-posted trail veers to the right. In a short distance bear to the left (east) to reach another yellow-capped post.

At a major junction turn left to follow a wide track, the route being confirmed by another yellow-capped post. Go through areas of new plantation and wide open space. As the yellow markers fork to the right, keep straight on, ignoring tracks to the left and the right. Coincidentally, we are now following a yellow cyclists' waymark. At a major junction, now about 1¼ miles from the visitor centre, take the second track on the left, soon confirmed as another part of the trail based on Warren Lodge along which we started.

Bend to the left and pass a huge cleared area on the right to reach Rishbeth Wood and the Forest Drive. Turn right at once to pass a barrier, staying with the red route as it rises gently, soon reaching a junction with red and yellow signs. Turn left and walk to rejoin the outward route in a short distance. Continue round to the right to return to the Lodge and the car park.

High Lodge Visitor Centre

---

28. Castle Acre

Length: 6 miles. *(The extension to include West Acre adds about 1 mile).*

Summary: A generally level walk in the valley of the River Nar, to and from a
delightful village, almost all along good tracks and footpaths, with very
little use of public roads. A small extension of the route gives a visit to
the smaller village of West Acre.

Car Parking: Street parking in the middle of Castle Acre village. Grid reference
816152.

Maps: Ordnance Survey Pathfinders 880, Kings Lynn South /881, East
Dereham and Castle Acre, 1:25,000. Ordnance Survey Landranger
132, North West Norfolk, 1:50,000.

Tea Shops

Willow Cottage is a traditional tea shop with a pleasant outdoor
area. The teas listed on the menu all have some explanation of the
taste to be expected – encouraging for those willing to experiment
with different brews. Light lunches include traditional favourites
such as home made soup with locally baked bread, Welsh rarebit,
baked beans on toast, or a ploughman's lunch. Tea temptations are
lemon drizzle cake, coffee and walnut gateaux, and flapjacks. Bed
and breakfast is also available.

Open: 10.30am – 5pm daily every day but closed on Mondays except
Bank Holidays. Tel. 01760 755551.

Across on the other side of the Green can be found **Castle Gate Tea
Room** – good food is served here too, again in very pleasant sur-
roundings.

About the Area

Castle Acre is a very historic and attractive village with a great deal
of visitor interest, built at a strategic point where the ancient
Peddars Way crosses the River Nar. The huge flint keep of the castle
constructed by William de Warenne, son in law of William the Con-
queror, stands in ruins on a great motte (mound) close to the village
centre, which is largely within the line of the former outer bailey.
The castle is in the care of English Heritage.

The 11th-century Cluniac priory is found a short distance beyond the large 13th/15th-century church of St James. The substantial priory ruin has a glorious west front with decorated arches and a varied and interesting use of building materials, both local and imported from as far away as Caen in Normandy, a conspicuous display of the great wealth in this area at the time. During the summer the priory has a programme of events such as craft displays, sheepdog demonstrations and medieval theatre. The on-site visitor centre is unusually comprehensive in display and interpretation. The parish church is mainly of the 15th century, with soaring arcades and an old painted screen.

The priory ruin at West Acre is not open to the public but can be seen to some extent from a minor road. Nearby, West Acre Gardens, open to the public from March to mid November, have many unusual plants on display. The village also has an inn.

South Acre church of St George is 14th/15th century. Inside are a massive Norman font, tombs, brasses and a rare wooden figure.

The Walk

From Castle Acre village walk along Priory Road, with the parish church on the left. *At a 'T' junction turn left by the public conveniences to visit the priory ruins.*

Otherwise, turn right at the junction, then left in 60 metres at a 'Nar Valley Way' signpost to go along a stony lane. After a right-hand bend turn left in approximately 200 metres through a waymarked kissing gate.

A good grass path stays close to the modest River Nar until the woodland of the West Acre Estate is entered at a kissing gate. Squirrels and pheasants seem to be plentiful in this woodland. Leave the wood at an old iron gate to cross a rough meadow and go over a stream on a wooden footbridge. The large house to the left is Mill House. Cross the Nar on another bridge to reach a minor public road.

Turn right towards a ford and footbridge, but turn left immediately before the bridge to follow a clear footpath, initially quite close to the river. The way is straightforward to follow; as the tracks divide, keep to the wider. Join a more important track; turn sharp left, then right in a further 10 metres.

To visit West Acre village, turn right along the more important track and cross the river by the footbridge.

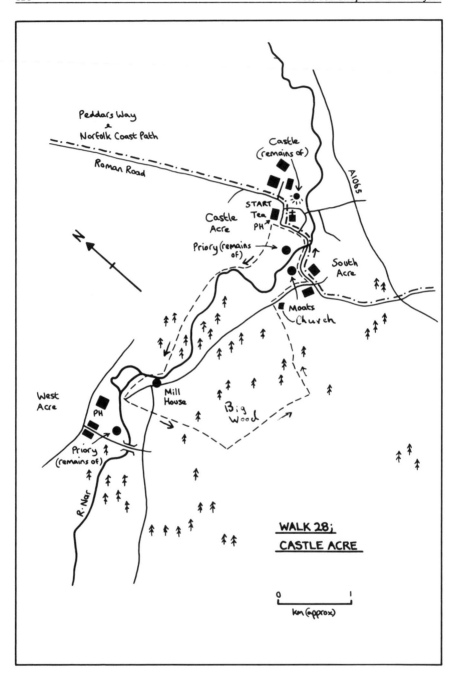

WALK 28;
CASTLE ACRE

After the right turn, follow a waymarked path along the edge of a field. Go straight across a public road to a broad, sandy, agricultural track with signpost, slightly uphill.

Pass the end of a tree belt, still rising. As the track bends sharply to the right, turn left along a 'road used as public path' along the bottom edge of a field. Go straight across a junction. The great fields of sugar beet and wheat are enlivened by field-edge poppies and ox-eye daisies, with busy butterflies.

Turn left at the next junction to pass an isolated house before reaching a large farm complex. As a wide driveway sweeps to the right, into the farm, walk straight on to join the road. Turn right for about 400m; over a gate on the left of the road part of an ancient moat can be seen. Pass the flint church of St George, South Acre and fork left at a 'Ford – unsuitable for motors' sign, then left again to pass a house named 'Little Brooms'.

Continue along an unsurfaced lane, with glimpses of the ruins of Castle Acre priory. Cross the river by the footbridge at a pretty spot, then rise along the surfaced road towards Castle Acre village. Reach the church then turn right, back to the village centre.

Castle Acre

29. Oxburgh Hall

Length:	Variable – 2½ miles maximum.
Summary:	A pleasing and easy walk in the woodland and parkland for those who want to stretch their legs as part of a visit to this National Trust owned stately home. For N.T. members entrance is, of course, free. With one exception, noted below, paths are good.
Car Parking:	Oxburgh Hall car park. Grid reference 743013.
Maps:	Ordnance Survey Pathfinder 900, Downham Market and Marham, 1:25,000. Ordnance Survey Landranger 143, Ely and Wisbech, 1:50,000.

Tea Shop

Following an exploration of the estate and perhaps prior to visiting this lovely house, a stop for refreshment is fully justified. Lunches and teas are available in The Old Kitchen – complete with old range. Great imagination together with skilful adaptation of old recipes has resulted in some unique dishes such as 'Rich man's stew with pot boars' – the latter being a kind of dumpling. 'Breads from the bothy' are served as platters with a variety of savouries – try the vinegared cockles served with crusty bread. Some of the tea specials on offer from The Bakehouse are date loaf and home made cakes. Drinks include tea, coffee, ginger or elderflower cordial. The tubs of ice cream are delicious.

Open: 11am - 5pm from 1st April (Easter if earlier) to the end of October. Closed on Thursdays and Fridays except in August when open every day. Also open on Saturdays and Sundays in March. Suggest checking in National Trust handbook or telephoning before visit if in any doubt. Tel. 01366 328258.

About the Area

Oxburgh Hall, at Oxborough, built in 1482, is a most attractive moated house with a fine Tudor gatehouse. The Hall is surrounded by lovely gardens, whilst the woodland and parkland provide a generous area for the walk set out below. Trees to be seen include alder, ash, beech, lime, oak, poplar and sweet chestnut. Inside the Hall there is a wealth of interest including hangings of needlework by Mary Queen of Scots, a 16th-century priest's hole, an armoury and wonderful views from the roof. Beside the Hall is St Mary's Chapel.

Oxburgh Hall

The Walk

The tracks available divide into two distinct areas. For a short walk head for 'My Lady's Wood'. Turn left on approaching the Hall from the car park, to head for a kissing gate. Do not go through, but keep close to the side of the tiny River Gadder. Do not cross the little draw-bridge on the left, but keep straight on, turning right by the weir to complete a clockwise circuit of this fine little wood, crossing several watercourses *en route*.

To return directly to the Hall gives a short walk of about half a mile.

To continue the walk to the larger area of Home Covert, the in-tended link from My Lady's Wood is to turn left along a not very dis-tinct footpath just before a bridge over the River Gadder, perhaps

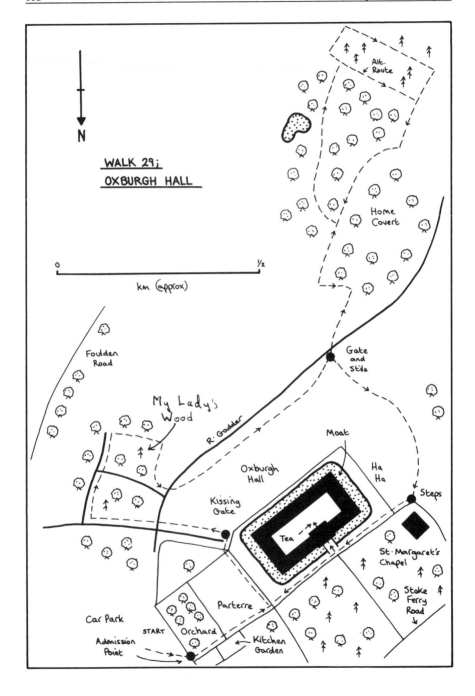

N

WALK 29;
OXBURGH HALL

0 _____ ½
km (approx)

Alt.
Route

Home
Covert

Foulden
Road

My Lady's
Wood

R. Gadder

Gate
and
Stile

Oxburgh
Hall

Moat

Ha
Ha

Steps

Kissing
Gate

Tea

St. Margaret's
Chapel

Stoke
Ferry
Road

Car Park

Admission
Point

START

Orchard

Parterre

Kitchen
Garden

90% of the way round the circuit in the wood. The river is then crossed on another bridge and the route across the rough meadow in front of the Hall keeps close to the river, heading for a gate and stile which gives access to the woodland of Home Covert. However, this path across the meadow appears to be little used and is not really defined on the ground.

Fine if you are wearing boots and are accustomed to rough walking, but *many will prefer to walk a little extra distance by returning to the Hall and walking round to the steps which are referred to in the return section. From the steps go directly to the gate and stile.*

In either case, from the gate/stile take the well-used path rising through the Covert and complete either the longer or the shorter of the two circuits available. Return to the gate/stile and head for the steps close to St Mary's Chapel for tea at the Hall and the return to the car park.

---

30. Downham Market

Length: 6¾ miles.

Summary: An outward walk across almost level agricultural land, a stroll through
                 Downham Market, urban and suburban, and a return along the side of
                 the Great Ouse River which gives the flavour of real Fenland walking.
                 Three straightforward stiles. First class paths and tracks.

Car Parking: Large roadside parking area opposite the Heron Inn, which is situated
                 on a minor road from Stowbridge to Stow Bardolph, between the two
                 main waterways. Grid reference, 604070.

Maps: Ordnance Survey Pathfinders 899, Wisbech (south) and 900
                 Downham Market and Marham, 1:25,000. Ordnance Survey
                 Landranger 143, Ely and Wisbech, 1:50,000.

Tea Shop

Considering the size of Downham Market, it proved surprisingly difficult to find a suitable place for tea. Eventually a visit to the Tourist Information Centre was made and 'The Tea Kosy' was suggested. This is a basic tea shop – no frills but clean acceptable, and busy. There is a choice of coffee from instant, cappucino, cafetiere, and a choice of tea including Earl Grey, Darjeeling, Assam, or herbal. Savouries include salads, sandwiches, and hot dishes. Suggestions for tea are scones, toast, crumpets, and cakes; for something hot and tasty try the bacon rolls.

Open: 9.30am to 5pm all the year. Closed Wednesdays and Sundays. Tel. 01366 383872.

About the Area

Fenland is a remarkable area with its huge expanse of approximately 1500 square miles of fertile agricultural land, created over the centuries by the progressive drainage of the previous ponds and marshes. From medieval times man has sought to bring areas of this land into use, most notably in the mid 17th century, when Vermuyden and other Dutch engineers dug massive drainage channels such as the

Clock at Downham Market

Bedford River (now Old Bedford River), 21 miles from Earith to Denver, the New Bedford River and the Forty Foot drain. A complex system of dykes and drains was linked to the waterways and hundreds of pumps – wind, steam, oil and electricity powered over the centuries – raised the water from the sinking fields into these waterways. It is an area of strongly individual character, thinly populated, flat as a pancake and with huge uninterrupted skies. Many people hate it but there are those who would live nowhere else.

Downham Market is a small, busy town with a Friday market, standing on rising ground on the eastern edge of the fens. The town centre has an interesting clock tower and a 15th-century church. The railway station has services on the line from Kings Lynn to Ely and beyond. To the south west Denver Sluice is one of the great features of modern fen drainage; nearby is a restored windmill, open to the public.

One mile to the west of Downham Market, at Hermitage Hall, the collection amassed by Eric St John Foti is truly remarkable and well worth seeking out but opening times are very limited and prior enquiry at the local Tourist Information Centre is advisable.

The Walk

Walk to the road and turn right. Cross the cut and immediately turn right through a small gate to walk along the top of a grassy embankment. Alongside is an elongated scrapyard, a remarkable place with a wonderful assortment of cars, caravans, boats, agricultural machinery, tractors and even the odd fire engine.

Cross a tiny stream then, in about 300 metres look out for a small white gate on the left. Descend the side of the embankment to this gate and, with suitable care, cross the railway line to a similar gate on the far side. A clear track goes through, believe it or not, another collection of scrap, strewn along the sides of the roadway. Proceed to a junction; turn right here, passing an isolated house. Silver birch and oak are plentiful in the woodland to the left of the track.

Turn sharp left at the end of the wood. Wimbotsham village is in view ahead.

To visit the village a simple detour to the left is all that is required.

At the next junction, turn right to take a broad farm track, with cultivated land on both sides. Go straight on at the next junction, soon bending to the left and rising gently. Kink left then right to head for Lower Farm and reach a public road, with a small layby and a waymark on a post.

Turn right to head along a track towards the left-hand edge of woodland. Bear left here towards the residential fringe of Downham Market. The path narrows; cross a footbridge over a stream and continue behind houses. At a major track turn left for 30 metres to reach a residential road. Turn right to walk towards the town centre along Wimbotsham Road, through modern suburban housing.

Ignore a left bend used by through traffic and carry on to a left turn at Bathcroft Close. Bear right to a footpath which leads directly into the town centre at Paradise Road. Turn right then, in 50 metres turn left through the Somerfield car park. The Tea Kosy Café is on the opposite side of the street at the far end of the car park (turn left).

After refreshment turn left from the café and walk down the street towards the railway station for almost half a mile. Go over the level crossing at the bottom; the adjacent station has what appear to be the original buildings in fair condition and a traditional signal box. Cross the cut on the road bridge and turn right at once at large gates and stile. The machinery of Denver Sluice is visible away to the left.

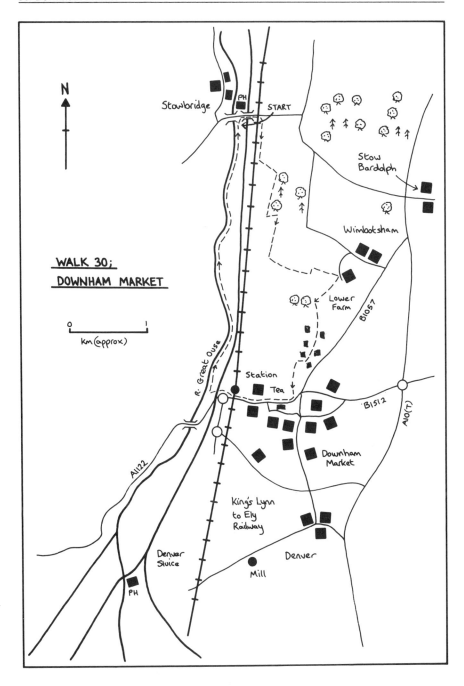

N

Stowbridge

PH

START

Stow
Bardolph

Wimbotsham

WALK 30;
DOWNHAM MARKET

0 _____ 1
km (approx)

Lower
Farm

B1057

R. Great Ouse

Station

Tea

B1512

A10(T)

Downham
Market

A1122

King's Lynn
to Ely
Railway

Denver
Sluice

Denver

Mill

PH

Follow a wide stony track rising to the top of the embankment by the Great Ouse River. Now is the opportunity to decide whether you are a fenland walker – three miles by the side of a great waterway under a huge wide sky, with the main interest focused on the bird life and probably with only a few sheep for company. If you like it, there is plenty more of the same to be sampled in this area. Stride out, passing a gate/stile; bridges over both waterways come into view and the public road is reached through 2 small gates. Turn right to return to the car park.

Tea Shop Walks - Spreading everywhere!

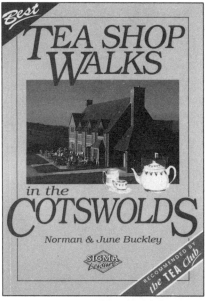

The Sigma Leisure Best Tea Shop Walks series includes:

Cheshire
The Chilterns
The Cotswolds
Dorset
The Lake District, Volume 1
The Lake District, Volume 2
Lancashire
Leicestershire & Rutland
North Devon
The Peak District
Shropshire
Snowdonia
South Devon & Dartmoor
Staffordshire
Surrey & Sussex
Warwickshire
The Yorkshire Dales

Each book costs £6.95 and contains an average of 25 excellent walks – far better value than any other competitor!

In case of difficulty, or for a free catalogue, please contact:
SIGMA LEISURE, 1 SOUTH OAK LANE, WILMSLOW, CHESHIRE SK9 6AR.

Phone: 01625-531035
Fax: 01625-536800.
E-mail: info @sigmapress.co.uk
Web site:
http//www.sigmapress.co.uk

VISA and MASTERCARD welcome.

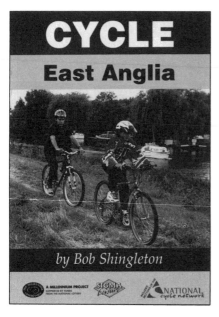

CYCLE EAST ANGLIA
Bob Shingleton

Cycling suits East Anglia - its fortuitous combination of quiet by-ways, timeless landscape, flat terrain and moderate climate is just made for the two-wheeled traveller. With rides in classic areas such as Cambridge and the Norfolk Broads, these 25 routes ranging from 10 to 35 miles help you get the best cycling out of the region - as well as providing notes on everything from Sustrans' admirable National Cycle Network to Chris Boardman's Norfolk-designed gold medal-winning bike. A substantial resource book for cyclists and an interesting read when you're not on your bike.

£6.95

All of our books are available through your local bookseller.

In case of difficulty, or for a free catalogue, please contact:

SIGMA LEISURE, 1 SOUTH OAK LANE, WILMSLOW, CHESHIRE SK9 6AR.

Phone: 01625-531035; Fax: 01625-536800.
E-mail: info@sigmapress.co.uk.

Web site: http//www.sigmapress.co.uk

VISA and MASTERCARD welcome.